More CUSTOM *Slipcovers*

Easy to Make & Snug-Fitting

Marge Jones

Schiffer
Publishing Ltd

4880 Lower Valley Road • Atglen, PA 19310

Library of Congress Control Number: 2014946593

Type set in Amplitude/Belwe/Bickly Script/Agenda

ISBN: 978-0-7643-4681-1
Printed in China

Published by Schiffer Publishing, Ltd.
4880 Lower Valley Road
Atglen, PA 19310
Phone: (610) 593-1777; Fax: (610) 593-2002
E-mail: Info@schifferbooks.com

For our complete selection of fine books on this and related subjects, please visit our website at www.schifferbooks.com. You may also write for a free catalog.

This book may be purchased from the publisher. Please try your bookstore first.

We are always looking for people to write books on new and related subjects. If you have an idea for a book, please contact us at proposals@schifferbooks.com.

Schiffer Publishing's titles are available at special discounts for bulk purchases for sales promotions or premiums. Special editions, including personalized covers, corporate imprints, and excerpts can be created in large quantities for special needs. For more information, contact the publisher.

To my mom and dad, Shirley and Lowell, who
have since passed. I know they would be so proud.
They were great conveyers of their knowledge and
patience — teaching me sewing, working with
power tools, and sharing their creativity …

Thank You

To my husband, Walt, who displayed loving patience and cooked many meals while I spent hundreds of hours compiling the manuscript ...

Thank You

To our siblings and friends who constantly gave me encouragement.

To our children—Tonya, Mark, Heidi, Angela—and their families for all their loving support.

To my dear friends, Paula Ryan, Lois Hottinger, and Benita Burgess, for all the time they devoted editing the manuscript.

Thank You

A special thank you to my clients who allowed me to photograph their slipcover projects.

Contents

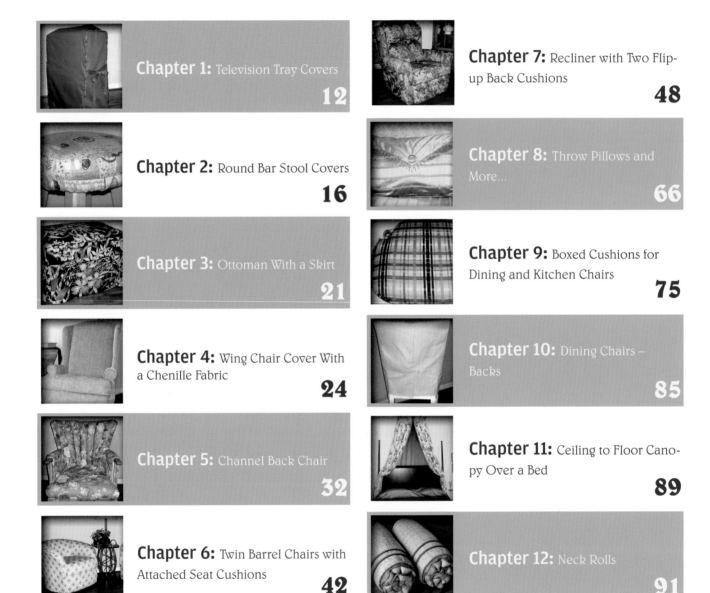

Introduction

With the success of my first book, *Marge's Custom Slipcovers*, it was only natural to start working on this one. It sure has been interesting, educational, challenging, and rewarding working on the manuscripts. I wrote the books with you, the reader, in mind, and I do hope you find them inspirational and useful when you start your own custom slipcover project.

Through my learning years, I've developed a "can do" attitude, and if you put your mind to it, you can do it too. Don't give up, keep on persevering. If you have furniture that needs to be spruced up and don't dare to use decorator fabric, I would suggest using bedsheets or muslin for your first slip-covering attempt. To cut down on your expense even more, you can purchase bedsheets at most thrift stores and yard sales — and then it's practice, practice, practice.

Being raised with three siblings and living in a small town, I learned at an early age to be inventive and creative. I have always been a firm believer in refurbishing, repurposing, restyling, and just simply making something old look new again. This came from my Mom and Dad, who were both very talented and creative. Dad built many boats and had a small salt-water fishing lure business.

When I was old enough and tall enough to run the ban saw and drill press, I helped with the fishing lure business. When Dad worked on the last two boats, my brother and I were his helping hands when needed. Mom was a great teacher when it came to my learning to sew. With her sewing talent, she would make most all of our clothes. When I got old enough, I started to help her with the family sewing. This is where my "can do" attitude, creativity, and acquaintance with power tools got their start. My parents were very inspirational and great conveyers of knowledge.

My upholstery and slip-covering talent got started when I was a young married mom with three kids. We had bought an older motor home that needed redecorating. With scissors, pins, tape measure, and a brocade fabric I purchased for $1 per yard in hand, I started covering the mattresses. It was then on to the dinette area, but I stopped at the two front bucket seats because I really didn't think I could do them. A family member said, "Of course you can." I gave it some thought and started to build my self-confidence. With that encouragement, I tackled one seat at a time. I detached the seat cover and marked all adjoining seams. I then took the seat cover apart and laid all the pieces right-side up on the fabric, cut them out, and transferred the marks onto the fabric. I kept sewing and trying the cover on the seat until it was finished. Well, by then my pride was soaring pretty high. The second bucket seat took me about half the time.

My next project was upholstering a used sleeper sofa, then the rest of our living room furniture, and the rest, as they say, "is history." I placed an ad in our local paper, "Upholstering, your fabric, my labor," and my new business was off and running. My first client's chair took me one whole week and, again, my pride was soaring. After a few weeks, my small business was on a roll. During this time, I had many phone calls inquiring about slipcovers. With much thought about my ability to reupholster, I figured slip-covering couldn't be that hard — and it really isn't.

I have written this book with simple, illustrated instructions. Hopefully, it will aid you with your first slip-covering project. For your first project, I recommend choosing a simple piece of furniture. After you have completed it, then move on to one a bit more detailed. All the while, you will be learning and building your self-confidence. Good luck ... I know you can do it.

Thank you for choosing my books.

Marge Jones

How Much Fabric Will You Need?

Check the following charts for the amount of fabric needed for your slip-covering project. Keep in mind that large repeats require extra fabric. Fabrics that have a nap (i.e., brushed cotton and velvet) also require extra fabric. It's always better to purchase a little extra fabric than not enough. With extra fabric, you can make accessories, such as arm protectors, head protectors, and throw pillows. If you don't purchase enough fabric for your slipcover, you may not be able to purchase more with the same dye lot.

Most fabric stores have yardage charts for your convenience. I have found the charts are only estimated guides. Your fabric needs will depend on many things: width of fabric, pattern repeat, nap (if any), size of furniture, style of skirt (if any), and arm protectors and throw pillows if desired.

Yardage requirements are approximate and will vary depending on pattern.

**TV Tray/
Stand Cover**
3 Yards

Channel Back Chair
6 yards (no skirt)

Two Neck Rolls
1 yard depending on size of roll

One Round Bar Stool Cover
.75 yards per stool

Barrel Back Chair
6 yards (no skirt)

**Three-Piece Sectional
with Skirt**
38-40 yards (solid fabric)

Ottoman
3 Yards Tailored Skirt

Recliner
8-9 yards depending on pattern
repeat

Pillow Shams
1.5 yards per sham

Wing Chair/No Skirt
about 7-8 yards depending on nap
or pattern repeat

Kitchen Chair Boxed Cushion
1.25 yards, Velcro tabs, cording on
the bias

Chapter 1

Television Tray Covers

1 This cover for a set of television trays on a stand is a decorative solution. Measure from the floor up to the top of the handle and down to the floor on the opposite side. Now, add 6" to this measurement.

2 Measure across the stand at the widest point and add 3" to 4".

3 Use double-sided tape to temporarily hold the fabric in place on the wooden frame where the fabric will touch the wood. When the seams are completely pinned, the tape can be removed.

NOTE: If you have any question about harming the finish with tape, do a tape test by placing and removing the tape in an inconspicuous place.

4

Using the previous measurements, cut the front/back fabric. If your fabric has no design, cut one piece. Fold the length of fabric in half, end to end, and mark both folded edges with pins. Unfold and lay the fabric, wrong-side out, over tray stand. Align center markings with the handle ends as shown. Allow the extra length of fabric to lie on the floor. The extra fabric will create the hem. Measure the end width at the widest point and add 3".

5

If using a patterned fabric, center design in the middle of the back/front, and cut two pieces. Place back and front fabric cuts, right sides together, and stitch a .5" seam on the top edge. Align seam on top of the tray stand handle.

Measure the height of the tray stand's end at the highest point and add 4".

6

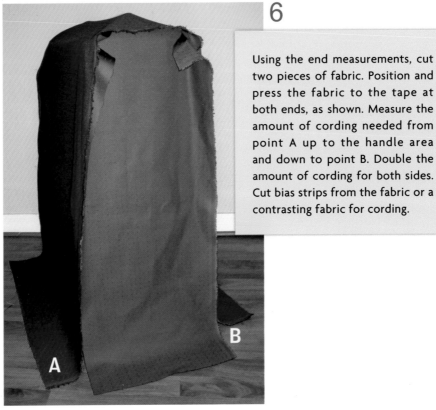

Using the end measurements, cut two pieces of fabric. Position and press the fabric to the tape at both ends, as shown. Measure the amount of cording needed from point A up to the handle area and down to point B. Double the amount of cording for both sides. Cut bias strips from the fabric or a contrasting fabric for cording.

NOTE: If the fabric has a design or a nap, there will be a seam at the top of the handle.

14

7

On top, at each end of the handle, make a dart. (Fold out and pin extra fabric.) Pin cording into the two end seams. Slide the cover off and sew it together. Check the seams. Trim excess fabric from the seam and zigzag or serge. Turn cover right-side out and slip it on the TV stand. Now it is time to finish the bottom edge.

8

The excess fabric at the bottom can simply be turned up and hemmed, or cording can be added to the bottom edge. At floor level, pin cording seam allowance to lower edge of cover. Sew cording and trim away extra fabric, leaving about a .75" seam allowance. Serge or zigzag cut edges of seam allowance. Now, press seam allowance to the wrong side. Finish lower edge by top-stitching about .5" from the cording on right side of the cover.

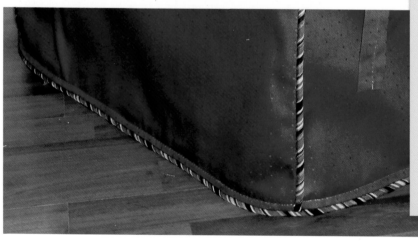

NOTE: For a final decorative touch, ties were added to the ends after project was initially completed.

Chapter 2

Round Barstool Covers

This style bar stool has a circular seat and can easily accommodate a padded, elasticized seat cushion. The underside of the cushion has a Velcro® closure for easy removal of the foam insert.

1

Trace around the top of the barstool with chalk, allowing a seam allowance, and cut the fabric.

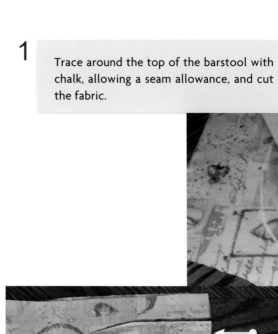

DIAMETER

2

For the underside Velcro closure, cut two half circles 3" wider than half the top's diameter. Cut the three extra inches straight (see white arrows).

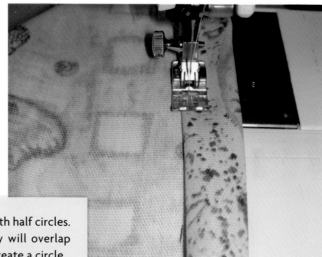

3

Hem the straight edges of both half circles. Leave enough width so they will overlap each other by about 1" and create a circle.

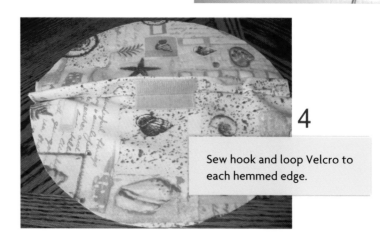

4

Sew hook and loop Velcro to each hemmed edge.

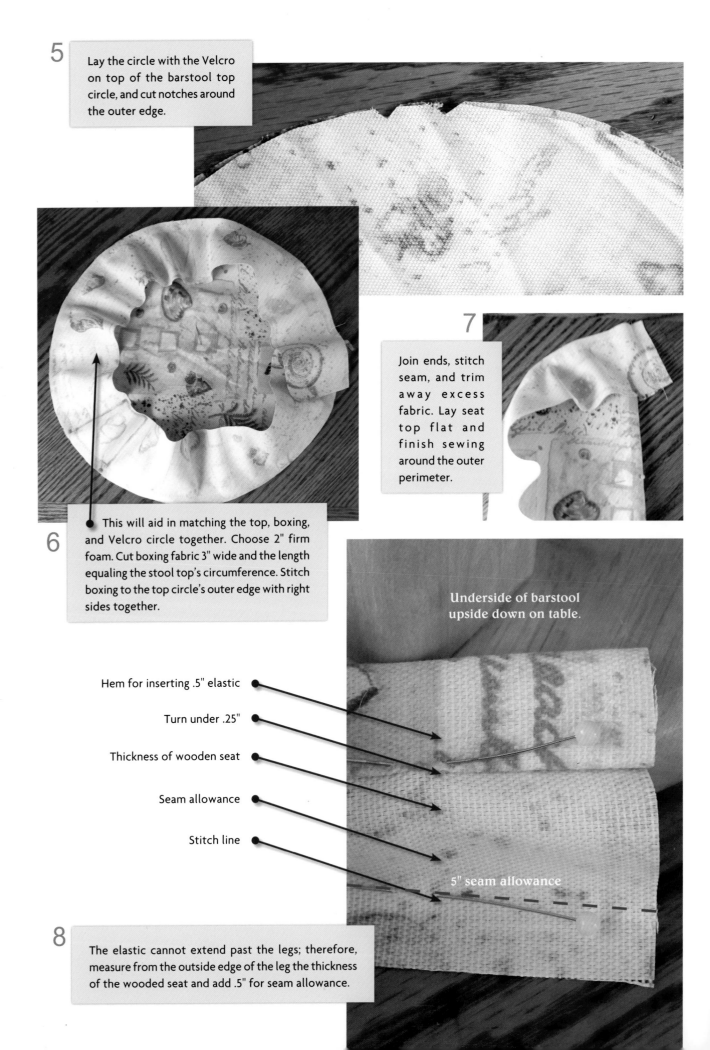

5 Lay the circle with the Velcro on top of the barstool top circle, and cut notches around the outer edge.

6 This will aid in matching the top, boxing, and Velcro circle together. Choose 2" firm foam. Cut boxing fabric 3" wide and the length equaling the stool top's circumference. Stitch boxing to the top circle's outer edge with right sides together.

7 Join ends, stitch seam, and trim away excess fabric. Lay seat top flat and finish sewing around the outer perimeter.

Underside of barstool upside down on table.

Hem for inserting .5" elastic

Turn under .25"

Thickness of wooden seat

Seam allowance

Stitch line

5" seam allowance

8 The elastic cannot extend past the legs; therefore, measure from the outside edge of the leg the thickness of the wooded seat and add .5" for seam allowance.

NOTE: When measuring this odd-shaped area, use a scrap of fabric or a flexible measuring tape. A steel measuring tape will not hug the area well enough.

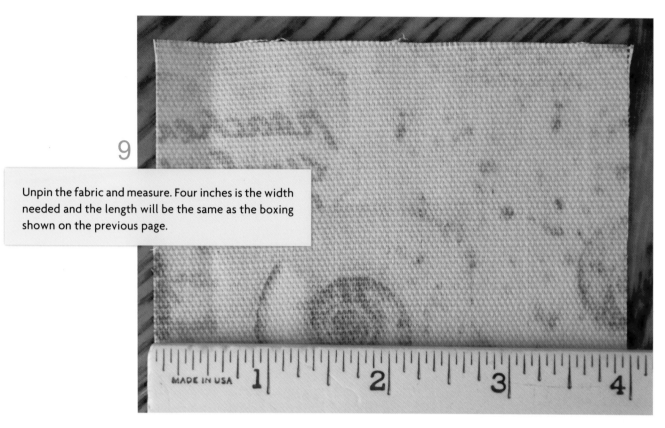

9

Unpin the fabric and measure. Four inches is the width needed and the length will be the same as the boxing shown on the previous page.

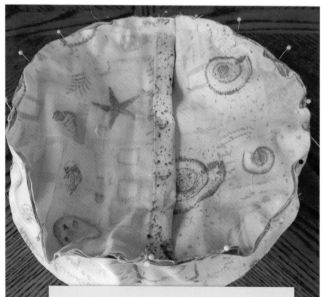

10 Sew the wrong-side of the elastic band to the right-side of the Velcro circle. The hem for the elastic will be completed later.

11 Match the notches and pin cushion boxing to the Velcro closure circle. Sew together, following the stitch line that attaches the elastic band to the Velcro closure circle. Turn right-side out and hem the lower edge of the elastic band, leaving a short opening for insertion of the .5" elastic.

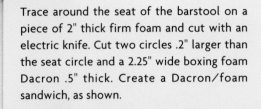

12

Trace around the seat of the barstool on a piece of 2" thick firm foam and cut with an electric knife. Cut two circles .2" larger than the seat circle and a 2.25" wide boxing foam Dacron .5" thick. Create a Dacron/foam sandwich, as shown.

13

Staple the Dacron boxing to the Dacron circles. If your barstools are being used outside near saltwater, I suggest using stainless steel staples and either hand-sewing or spray-gluing the Dacron together.

Measure the amount of elastic needed to fit around the top of the bar stool snugly. Thread elastic in the short opening in the hem; continue threading through the entire hem and out the short opening. Now, stitch across elastic ends to secure and place the seat cover on the bar stool.

NOTE: To thread elastic in a hemmed area, be sure that you use a large safety pin.

14

Open Velcro closure and insert Dacron-covered foam into your completed stool cover. Close Velcro closure.

Chapter 3

Ottoman With a Skirt

Before

After

Before

After

NOTE: When slip-covering, place fabric right-side facing furniture, unless otherwise mentioned. Cut bias strips for cording.

1

Measure length and width of the top and add 3" to each measurement. Cut fabric and, with right-side facing down, anchor pin it to top of the ottoman.

Measure and cut four strips of fabric for boxing — two ends and two sides. Anchor pin all boxing strips into place and join the boxing strips at each corner.

BOXING

2

Pin the cording into the seam, joining the top and boxing. Remove anchor pins, slide slipcover off, and sew all seams.

3

Turn cover right-side out and place it on the ottoman. Check the fit and make any adjustments.

4

With a ruler or yardstick, mark the same height around the ottoman for the skirt cording. Cut four strips of fabric for the skirt, allowing for seam allowances and hem.

5

The depth of the hem is a personal choice. Determine the hem on the weight of the fabric.

NOTE: If the slipcover fabric is heavy, serge or zigzag the raw edge and turn up the hem only once for less bulk. Use a 2" double hem if fabric is lightweight.

Chapter 4

Wing Chair Cover With a Chenille Fabric

The finishing touches to these twin chairs (below) are installing the zippers and making the cushions. Most of the instructions for "Boxed Cushions" in Chapter 9 can be applied to the cushion-making process here.

1

The fabric used to cover these chairs is chenille with a nap. Since the fabric design is a very small diamond pattern, no horizontal or vertical matching is necessary. *Note: When using a fabric that has a nap, all pieces must be cut in the same direction.*

Measure the height and width of the inside back. Cut the fabric and anchor pin it in place with the right side of the fabric toward the chair.

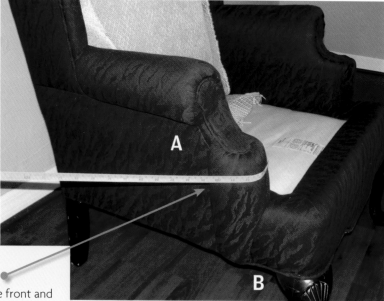

2

WIDTH: Measure the inside arm from back/arm joint towards the front and around the outside of the vertical arm roll. Add 5" extra for tucking in the back/arm joint and the outside arm seam allowance.

HEIGHT: Measure the height of the arm from the outside bottom of the vertical roll (B) up and overtop roll of the arm to point (A). Allow an extra 4".

3

Cut two pieces of fabric and anchor pin them onto each arm. At seat level, fold up the extra fabric at the arm's front lower curve.

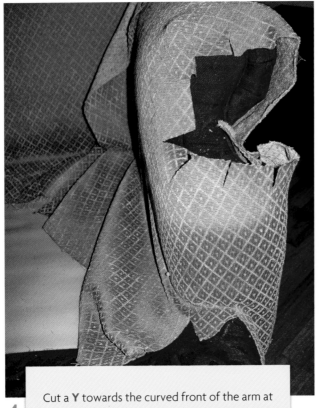

4 Cut a **Y** towards the curved front of the arm at seat level. When you cut close to the arm, cut a little at a time — do not over-cut.

5 Ease the fabric on the right-side of the cut, towards the outside of the vertical roll, and anchor pin into place.

Repeat these steps on the opposite arm.

6 Measure the height and width (at the widest point) of the inside wing and add 3" to 4" to both dimensions. Cut the fabric to size.

7 Smooth and anchor pin the inside wing fabric into place. As you smooth and pin fabric towards the outside of the wing, there will be excess fabric. Small darts need to be pinned to take care of the excess fabric. *Note: These darts should face up. When the finished slipcover is turned right side out and put on the chair, the darts will face down and will not be dust collectors.*

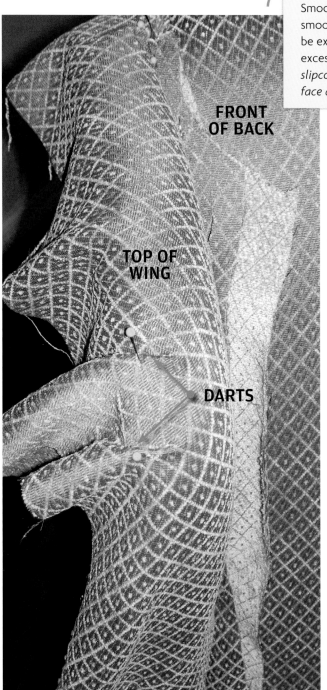

FRONT OF BACK

TOP OF WING

DARTS

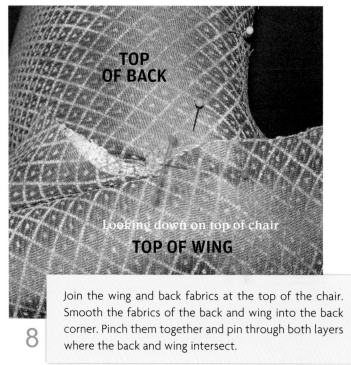

TOP OF BACK

Looking down on top of chair

TOP OF WING

Join the wing and back fabrics at the top of the chair. Smooth the fabrics of the back and wing into the back corner. Pinch them together and pin through both layers where the back and wing intersect.

8

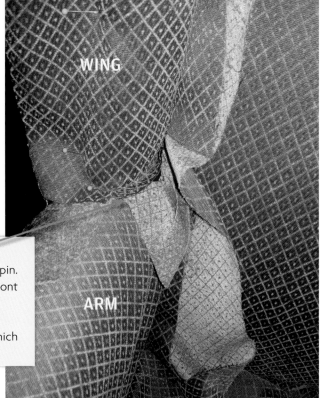

WING

ARM

9

Join the lower wing and arm fabrics. Pinch the two fabrics together, following the manufacturer's seam lines, and pin. Cut the fabric where necessary to ease fabrics around the front base of the wing.

Pin to the back corner of the chair plus 3" for the gusset, which will be used for tucking.

10

After the wing and arm are pinned together, join the back fabric and wing/inside arm fabrics. Smooth all fabrics into the back corner of the chair. Now, pinch both fabrics together and pin about 2" away from the back corner. Pin from the top of the chair, down towards the seat. This will create a long gusset/pocket to be tucked in.

When you reach 2" above the seat, angle in 2" towards the chair frame and then angle out 45 degrees towards the center of the chair decking.

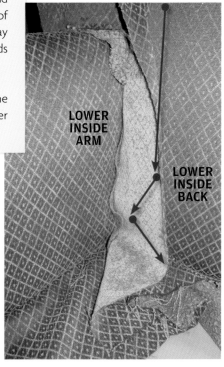

LOWER INSIDE ARM

LOWER INSIDE BACK

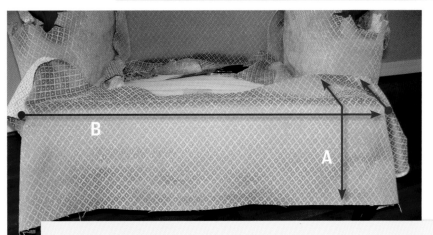

B

A

11

(A) Measure the front under the cushion area from lower arm at seat level to the bottom front of the chair at the lowest point and add 4".

(B) Measure width of seat from vertical arm roll across front to the opposite vertical arm roll and add 4".

Cut and anchor pin fabric in place, smoothing fabric around both front corners to the front edge of both vertical arm rolls.

12

Pin this seam down the outside of the chair next to the vertical roll following the manufacturer's seam line.

13

Pin bottom arm and seat fabric together. Clip and ease fabric around the front curve of the arm. Fold and pin out excess fabric at the seat front corners.

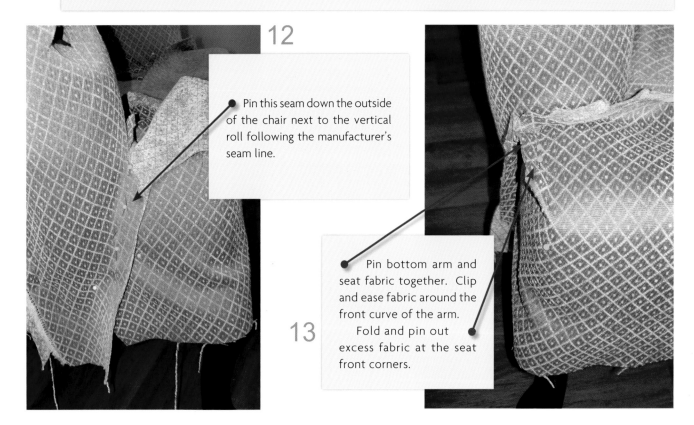

14

Measure the height and width (at the widest point) of the outside wing and add 3" to both measurements for the seam allowances. Cut the fabric and anchor pin it into place.

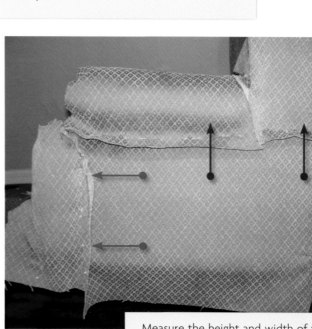

15

Measure the height and width of the outside arm and add 3" to both measurements. Cut and anchor pin fabric into place.

Now, join vertical arm roll fabric to outside arm fabric (see red arrows) and pin the underside of the rolled arm and lower edge of wing to the top of the outside arm fabric (see black arrows).

16

Measure the height and width of the back and add 3" to both measurements. Cut and anchor pin back fabric into place.

One back corner will be left open for the zipper. This is personal preference. The back corner seam, without the zipper, will be pinned from the top of the chair down to the top of the leg. The zipper seam will be pinned about 2" to 3" at the top and the rest of the seam pinned open.

NOTE ABOUT ZIPPER OPENING:
If the back right corner is designated for the zipper while pinning, it will be on the back left corner when turned right-side out.

17

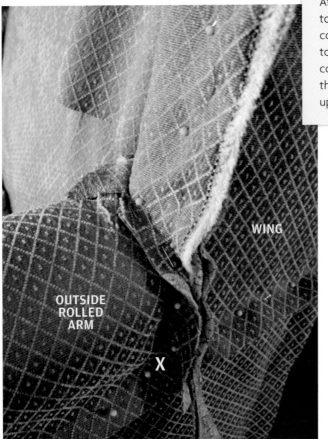

After all fabric pieces are cut and pinned into place, it is time to cut fabric bias strips for the cording. Estimate the amount of cording needed and cut the fabric strips on the bias. Sew them together end to end, cover the cording, and stitch close to the cord. Now, pin cording in-between the lower outside wing and the back of the outside rolled arm starting at the "X." Continue up the wing across the top of the wing to the back corner.

WING

OUTSIDE ROLLED ARM

X

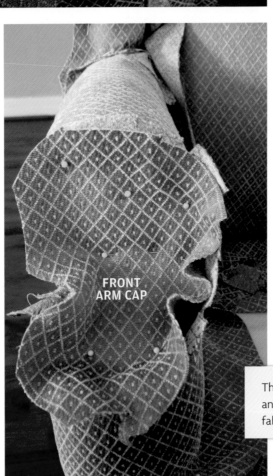

18

At the top back corner, clip the cording seam allowance and turn cording. Continue pinning across the top back. Repeat the same instructions at the opposite corner and across the top of the wing down to the same point as on the opposite side.

FRONT ARM CAP

19

The next step is to measure, cut, and anchor pin the front arm cap fabric into place.

20

Place the cording in-between the front arm cap fabric and the main arm fabric. Follow the corded edge of the existing arm. Now, clip the fabric and cording seam allowance where and when necessary.

NOTE: The remaining step in the pinning process is to check all seams, making sure pins are secure.

21

Remove the anchor pins only. Keep the folded zipper edges securely pinned. Now, remove the slipcover from the chair and begin sewing it together. After sewing all seams, trim and zigzag or serge all seam allowances, turn the slipcover right-side out, and slide it onto the chair.

NOTE: The chairs featured at the beginning of this chapter do not have skirts, but are finished with a single row of cording at the lower edge of the chair. Pin cording to the outside of the slipcover, following the manufacturer's cord line, and sew in place. Trim and zigzag or serge the seam allowance edge.

Chapter 5

Channel Back Chair

In my thirty-nine years of upholstering and creating custom slipcovers, I had never been asked to slipcover a channel back chair. When a customer said she had a channel back chair she wanted slip-covered, that set my brain spinning. I asked if she would allow me to use her chair as a teaching tool.

1

With a chair this old, the first step is to remove the under cloth from the underside of the chair to check the condition of the chair's frame and springs. Since the frame and springs seemed to be in relatively good condition, only the topside needed repairing.

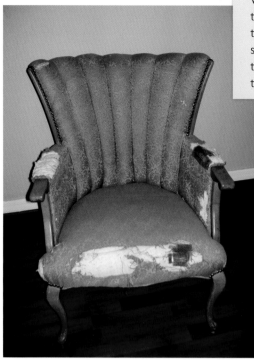

2

Dacron is used to smooth out the worn areas. Staple it to the outer underside of the arm, and then trim and staple the Dacron around the wood trim at the front edge of each arm. Smooth it downward to the seat's outer edge and staple to the lower arm frame.

NOTE: Use enough staples to keep the Dacron smooth, but not too many to make it bumpy.

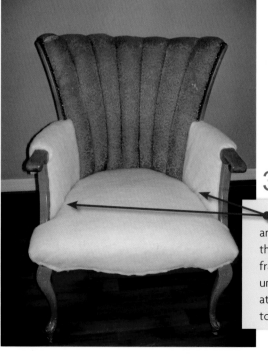

3

Measure the depth and width of the seat and cut a piece of Dacron to fit. Tuck it into the outer edge of the seat under the lower arm frame and staple the front lower edge to the underside of the chair. Trim the excess Dacron at each front corner and staple in place at the top of both legs.

4

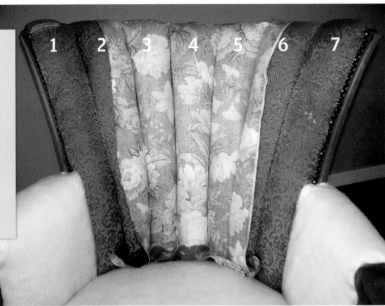

In between the five center channels (2, 3, 4, 5, and 6) are four deep vertical groves to tuck in the fabric. Therefore, covering these channels can be done with one piece of fabric. Measure the height and width of this area and include the amount of fabric needed for tucking in-between each of the channels. Now, cut fabric and fold in half to find center. Position the center of fabric on the center of channel (4) and anchor pin in place. Tuck fabric in between channels (4 and 5), (4 and 3), (3 and 2), and (5 and 6).

5

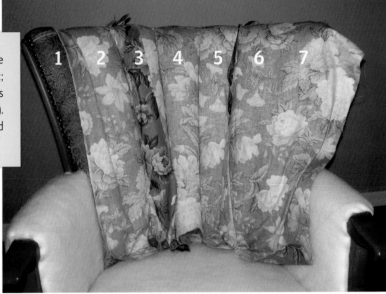

In between channels (1 and 2) and (6 and 7), there is not enough room for tucking in the fabric; therefore, the fabric pieces for these channels need to be seamed together (the seam will show). Now, join both of these channel sections (1 and 2, 6 and 7) to the center fabric.

6

After joining all of the channel pieces, clip around the arms of channels (1) and (7). Smooth the remaining fabric to the outside of the channels (as shown by the arrows) and anchor pin in place.

7

On the top outer corners of channels (1) and (7), create a dart with the excess fabric and lay the fold towards the center back.

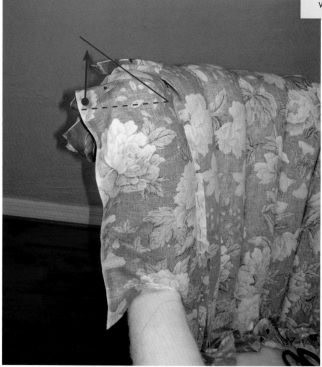

8 Measure the seat's depth and width, cut fabric, and position it on the seat. Anchor pin the seat fabric at the lower front of the chair and allow a 1" overhang for seam allowance.

Tuck the fabric on the seat back towards the bottom of the channels and fold extra seat fabric back onto the seat. Now, lay the bottom of the channel fabric on top of the folded back seat fabric. Match and pin both fabrics together about 2.5" to 3" away from the bottom edge of the channels. This creates a gusset/pocket, which will be tucked in-between the lower end of the channels and seat.

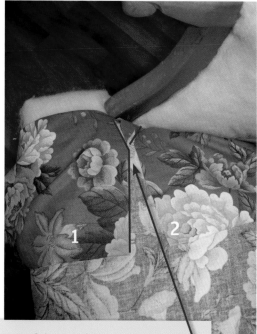

9 Fold this part of the seat fabric as shown and cut a "Y" to within .5" of the wooden trim on the arm. Section 1 will be smoothed in front of the wooden arm trim and down to the outside lower edge of the chair and section 2 will be joined to the lower arm fabric.

10 Smooth seat section 1 to the outside front corner of the seat, in front of the wooden arm trim, and anchor pin in place. If you need to clip the fabric to make it lay smoothly around the wood, clip a little at a time.

11

Measure the height and width of the center back section. Cut the fabric and then anchor pin the fabric in place.

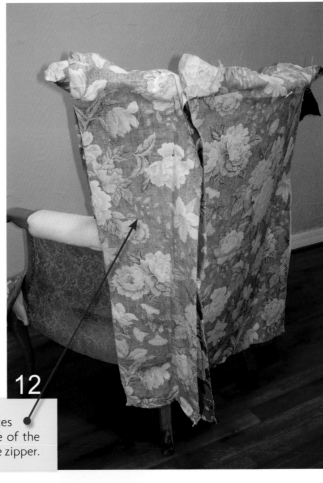

12

Measure the tall side/back height and width, cut two pieces of fabric, and anchor pin them in place, one on each side of the center back. One of the back seams will be left open for the zipper.

NOTE: If you leave the back right seam open, it will be on the back left when the slipcover is turned right-side out.

Measure the outside arm's width and height and cut two fabric pieces, one for each side. Anchor pin the two pieces in place and then join each piece to the tall side/back pieces.

13

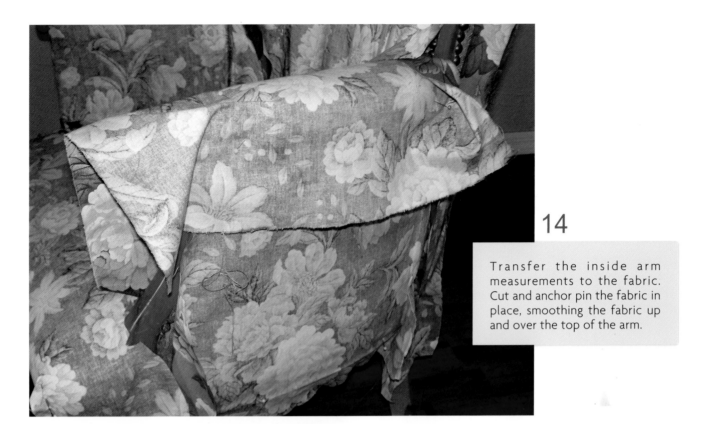

14

Transfer the inside arm measurements to the fabric. Cut and anchor pin the fabric in place, smoothing the fabric up and over the top of the arm.

15 Trim the fabric to within 1" of the wood/fabric/tack line at the front edge of the arm. Notice how the arm fabric tapers in near the wood trim. Now, create a dart with the excess fabric.

INSIDE ARM

16 Smooth the inside arm fabric towards the back of the arm. Clip where necessary to allow fabric to lay smoothly over the top curve of the arm's back portion.

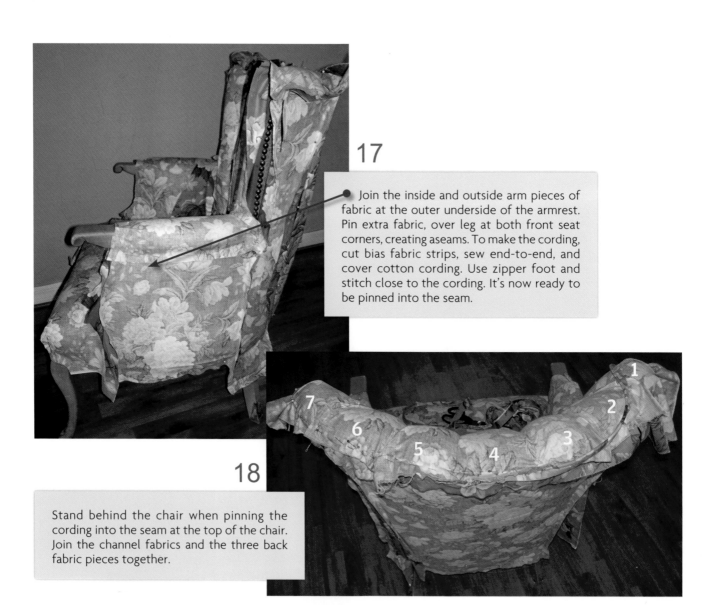

17

• Join the inside and outside arm pieces of fabric at the outer underside of the armrest. Pin extra fabric, over leg at both front seat corners, creating aseams. To make the cording, cut bias fabric strips, sew end-to-end, and cover cotton cording. Use zipper foot and stitch close to the cording. It's now ready to be pinned into the seam.

18

Stand behind the chair when pinning the cording into the seam at the top of the chair. Join the channel fabrics and the three back fabric pieces together.

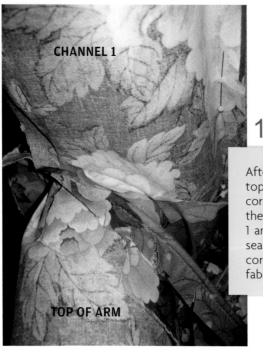

CHANNEL 1

TOP OF ARM

19

After pinning the cording across the entire top back, clip seam allowance at the top corners of channels 1 and 7. Pin down towards the arms, joining the outer edges of channels 1 and 7 and the tall side/back fabrics. Clip seam allowance at the top of the arm. Turn cording, and pin channel 1 and top of arm fabrics together with cording in-between.

20

Continue pinning the cording in the seam toward the seat.

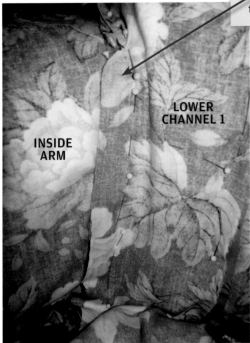

LOWER CHANNEL 1

INSIDE ARM

21

Following the exposed wood/fabric/tack line of the arm, pin cording to the right side of the fabric. Pin down the inside arm to the seat, clip, and turn cording. Continue pinning cording to the seat fabric, clipping where needed.

22

This image shows the cording pinned to the right side of the arm and seat fabrics, just in front of the wood trim.

23

Continue pinning the cording to the right side of the fabric, following the wood/fabric edge of the outside arm fabric. From this point to the bottom edge of the chair, the outside seat and the lower outside arm fabrics need to be joined with the cording in-between.

Check all seams, remove anchor pins, slide the slipcover off, and sew all seams together.

24

Slide slipcover back on the chair right-side out. Pin the zipper opening closed. Anchor pin the bottom edge of the slipcover to the lower edge of the chair.

25

Seam adjustments may need to be made. The area in between channels 6 and 7 was a bit too loose, so I made an adjustment to the seam.

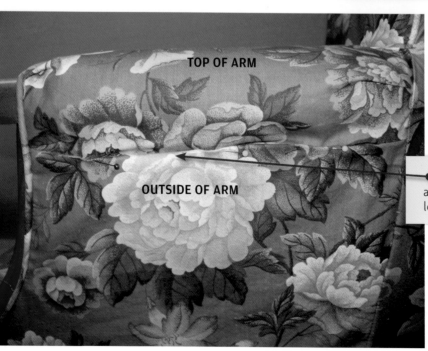

TOP OF ARM

OUTSIDE OF ARM

26

The seam joining the outside arm and inside arm fabrics was also a bit loose. Pin out the excess.

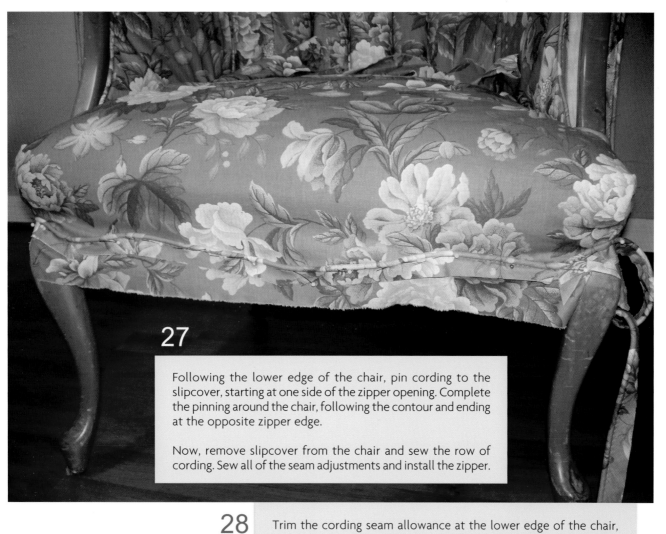

27

Following the lower edge of the chair, pin cording to the slipcover, starting at one side of the zipper opening. Complete the pinning around the chair, following the contour and ending at the opposite zipper edge.

Now, remove slipcover from the chair and sew the row of cording. Sew all of the seam adjustments and install the zipper.

28

Trim the cording seam allowance at the lower edge of the chair, and either serge or zigzag the cut edge. Install zipper in the zipper opening, and check all seams, making sure sewing adjustments have been completed.

Place slipcover on the chair and zip the zipper. Tuck all the extra fabric in between the channels and tuck down the extra seat/channel fabric in between the seat/lower channel area.

29

Use Velcro hook and loop fastener to secure lower cording seam allowance to the underside of the chair, or it can simply be stapled or tacked into position. The finishing touch to this slipcover is a row of decorative tacks securing the corded front arm edge in place.

Chapter 6

Twin Barrel Chairs with Attached Seat Cushions

When fitting two identical chairs with a patterned fabric, both should be pin fitted at the same time to ensure that the fabric patterns are in the same position.

Chairs with attached seat cushions will be fitted differently from other chairs featured.

1

Measure the width and height of center back, following the manufacturer's seams. Feel, with your hand, down between the back/lower arms and seat to determine how deep the slipcover fabric should go and then cut center back fabric and anchor pin it into place.

2

Measure and cut all four arm pieces of fabric and align them to the center back patterns.

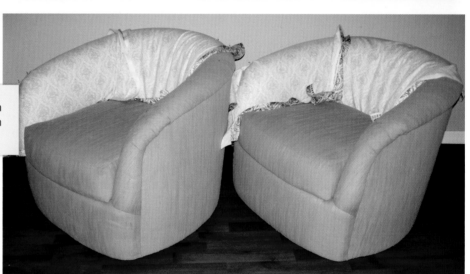

3

Use a leveling tool to make sure that the pattern is level and anchor pin in place. Repeat the same process on the remaining three arm fabric pieces.

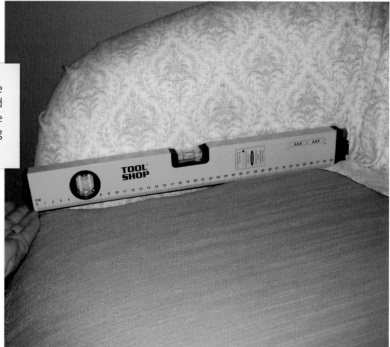

4

Measure the width and depth of the seat. Cut fabric pieces and anchor pin them into place. Now, cut two strips of fabric to cover the seat's boxing. Boxing is the band that creates the front and sides of the seat.

5

The boxing should be cut across the fabric from selvage to selvage. Fold boxing strip in half to find the center, and pin center of strip to center of the seat's boxing, matching the pattern to the seat fabric. Tuck the right and left ends of the strip in-between the lower arm and seat.

NOTE: The boxing does not reach around the entire seat. This is okay, as we will finish it later.

6

The zipper is going to be in the center back. Measure the back and outside arms, and then cut the fabric pieces and pin into place.

7

Measure, cut, and anchor pin fabric to the lower front of the chair. Join this fabric to the lower edge of the seat boxing fabric with cording in-between. To make the cording, follow directions in Chapter 5, "Channel Back Chair."

FRONT BOXING

8

Join center back and arm fabrics together with cording in-between. Start at the top of the chair and pin down past the top of the seat.

Now, we will complete the boxing. To do this, use the cut boxing fabric, tucking it in around the back of the seat. Join both boxing ends to one another, and then join the seat fabric and the top edge of the boxing with cording in-between.

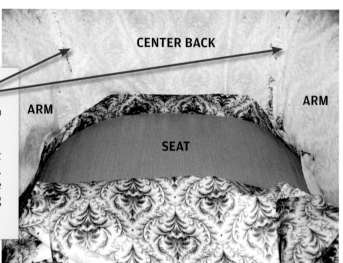

CENTER BACK

ARM

ARM

SEAT

9

Starting at a lower front corner, pin the cording into the outside seam. Continue pinning up the arm around the top outside edge, joining all adjacent pieces of fabric as you pin. Finish pinning to the opposite lower front corner. Now, join lower edge of the seat boxing to the lower edges of the center back and arms. Unpin the back center seam, slide the slipcover off, and begin sewing the seams.

10

Turn slipcovers right-side out and place them on the chairs. Make any adjustments now if necessary, and then trim, serge, or zigzag all seams.

11

Pin the cording to the right side of the slipcover following the bottom edge of the chair. Sew cording in place, trim the seams, and serge or zigzag. Install zipper in the zipper opening. This zipper installation is fairly easy: place the fabric folds over the zipper teeth, pin both sides, and stitch in place.

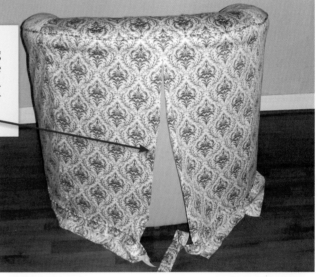

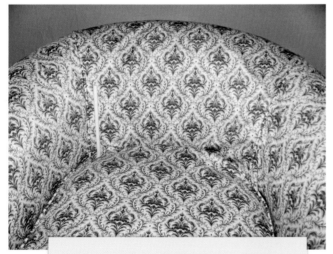

12 Place the slipcovers on the chairs for the final time. Tack, staple, or Velcro the cording seam allowance to the underside of the chair. Use a ruler or spatula to tuck the gusset/pocket in around the seat (as shown).

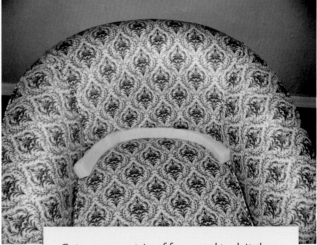

13 Cut a narrow strip of foam and tuck it deep into the gusset area. This will help hold the slipcover snugly in place.

Chapter 7

Recliner with Two Flip-up Back Cushions

After

Before

1 The first step in slip-covering a recliner is to dismantle it. Lift the lower edge of the back fabric. It is most likely secured in place with hook and loop Velcro. This recliner also has two bolts that need to be unscrewed in order to lift the back upward.

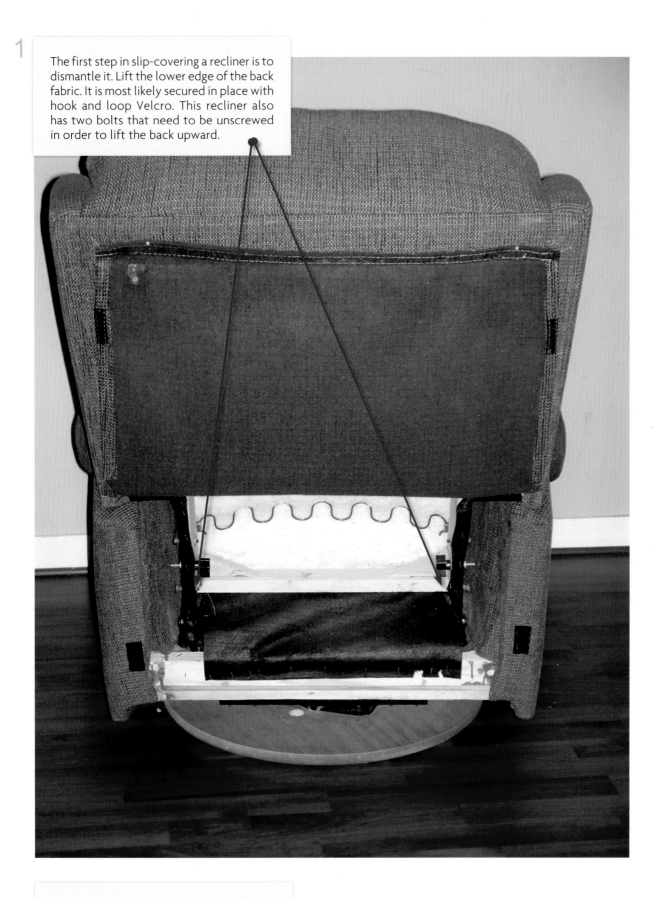

OPPOSITE PAGE: This recliner, with two flip-up attached back cushions, is the most detailed slipcover in this book.

2

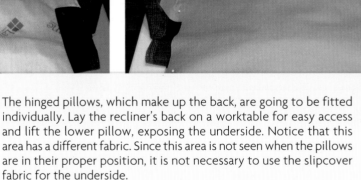

Some recliners have a lever on each side of the lower back. Insert a flat screwdriver under the lever and lift upward. Lift up evenly on both sides of the back, and it will slide up and away from the chair.

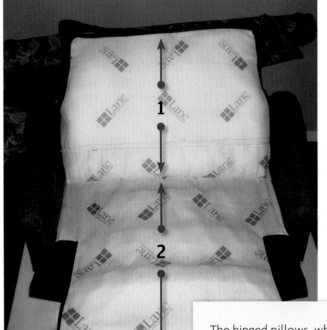

NOTE: Always add extra inches to your measurements for the seam allowance.

3

The hinged pillows, which make up the back, are going to be fitted individually. Lay the recliner's back on a worktable for easy access and lift the lower pillow, exposing the underside. Notice that this area has a different fabric. Since this area is not seen when the pillows are in their proper position, it is not necessary to use the slipcover fabric for the underside.

Measure the height and width of sections 1 and 2 and cut the fabric. Anchor pin these pieces in place.

4

Fold the lower back pillow to its original position, exposing the underside of the top pillow. Measure the height and width of the two sections. Cut the two underside fabrics and anchor pin them in place.

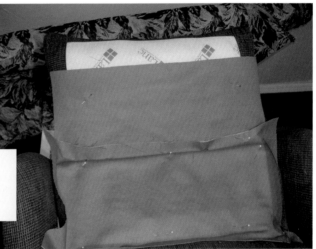

5

Pin the underside fabric pieces together following the manufacturer's seam lines.

6

Measure the height and width of the lower back pillow. Keep in mind the slipcover fabric's pattern, if any, and cut out the fabric piece. Anchor pin it, wrong-side out, to the pillow.

7   Repeat the same process on the top pillow. Measure from the top back edge of the chair around the pillow to meet the new underside fabric.

8

Since the small section on the underside of the top pillow may show, it should be covered with the slipcover fabric.

    Measure, cut, and anchor pin fabric into place. Since this piece is so small, pattern matching is not a concern.

9 Measure the ends of both hinged pillows. Cut two of each size and anchor pin them in place.

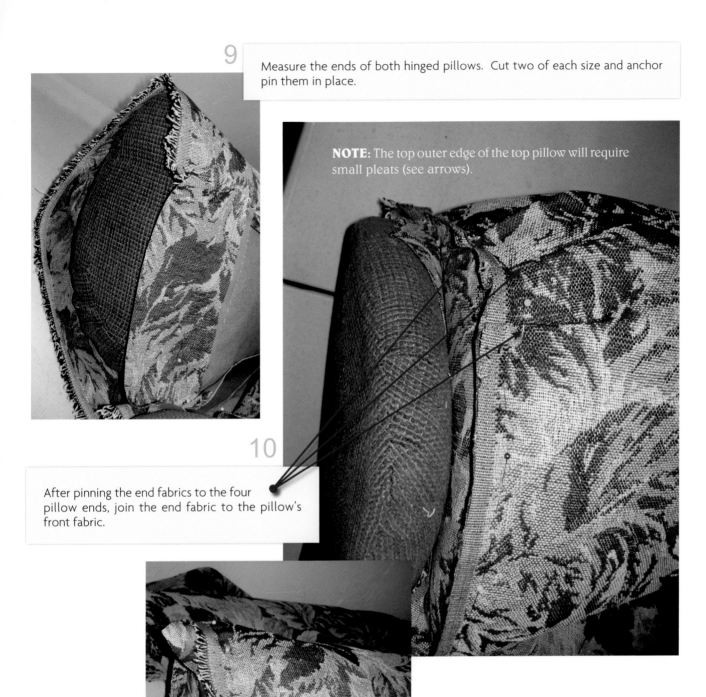

NOTE: The top outer edge of the top pillow will require small pleats (see arrows).

10 After pinning the end fabrics to the four pillow ends, join the end fabric to the pillow's front fabric.

11 Lift pillow and continue pinning seam towards the pillow's hinge. Remove anchor pins and sew all top pillow seams. Now, trim and zigzag, or serge, all seams.

12

Turn pillow cover right-side out and place on the chair. Check the fit and complete any adjustments at this time.

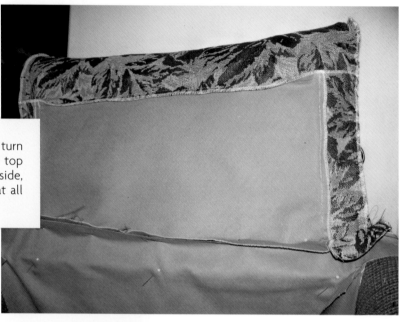

13

Remove the top pillow cover from the chair, turn it wrong-side out, and place it back on the top pillow. Lift top pillow, exposing the underside, and anchor pin fabrics into position. Repeat all previous steps on the lower pillow.

14

After sewing the lower pillow cover together, try it on right-side out and check the fit, and then place it back on the lower pillow wrong-side out. Join all underside fabrics together again.

15

This is a good time to place the back of the recliner on the chair to visually check the fit.

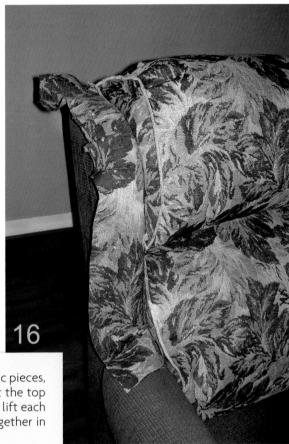

16

Measure the height and width of the inside wing and cut two fabric pieces, one for each inside wing. Anchor pin these pieces into place. At the top of the chair, pin the wing and top cushion fabrics together. Now, lift each hinged pillow, and pin the wing and the under-pillow fabrics together in a vertical line.

17

Measure and cut two pieces of fabric for both outside wings and anchor pin them into place.

Measure the height and width of the back of the recliner. Cut fabric and anchor pin it in place; now join the top pillow fabric and the top of the back fabric together. At the top of both back corners, pin the back and the outside wing fabrics together for about 3" to 4", allowing the remainder of the back fabric to hang free.

Lift the lower pillow and finish this area by pinning a small piece of fabric to the outer edge of the underside fabric, covering the area under the lower pillow. The edge that is folded back will have Velcro sewn on to it. Gently remove the pinned slipcover and sew all seams. Trim and zigzag, or serge, all seams.

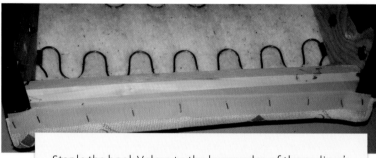

Staple the hook Velcro to the lower edge of the recliner's back, and then sew the loop Velcro to the corresponding part on the slipcover.

19

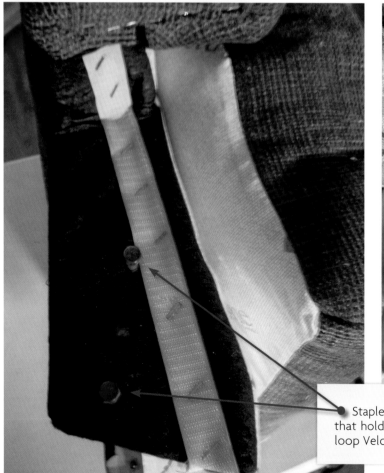

20

Staple the hook Velcro near the metal pins (see arrows) that hold the recliner's back in place, and then sew the loop Velcro to the corresponding area on the slipcover.

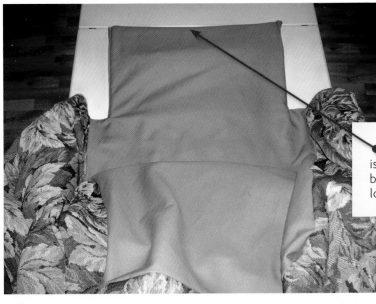

21

After all seams are sewn and checked, it is time to install the cover on the recliner's back. Secure the lower under-fabric to the lower edge of the back.

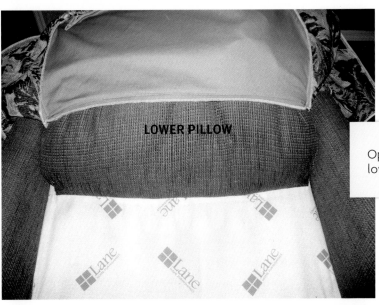

LOWER PILLOW

22

Open the lower pillow cover and insert the lower pillow.

NOTE: This will require a little pushing and tugging. Reach your hand inside the cover and adjust pillow into the corners.

23

Under the top pillow, place the underside fabric in position. Slide the slipcover wings over the recliner's wings and, after they are securely in position, pull towards the lower edge of the wing to remove any slack in the wing fabric. Secure the fabric with a staple. Repeat these same steps to insert the top pillow into its cover.

24

When securing the fabric to the lower end of the wing, do not use Velcro. It would require too many layers and would be too bulky. Instead, staple each layer as you fold the fabric, similar to wrapping a package.

25

Lower edge of wing: Fold outside wing fabric over inside wing fabric and staple through all layers. The back of the recliner is now complete.

26

Measure and cut the fabric for the seat surface. Keeping in mind the pattern placement, match it to the back pillow fabrics. After cutting the fabric, anchor pin it in place. Measure the height of the cushion's boxing, add 2" to 3" for seam allowances, and cut two strips. The first strip will be anchor pinned to the seat boxing; tuck the ends in-between the seat sides and lower inside arms.

27

Pin the second boxing strip across the seat's back boxing area and tuck in the ends the same way as the first strip. Join the two strips together in the middle of the side seat area.

28

Pin the seat's outer edge to the top edge of the two boxing strips. Remove the seat and sew it together. Trim and zigzag, or serge, the seam allowance.

NOTE: This seat piece will be worked on later in this chapter.

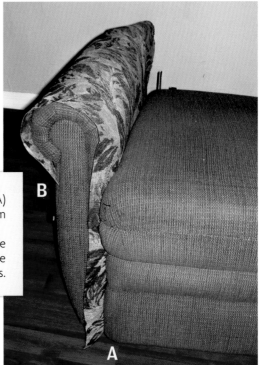

29

Measure the arm from the lowest inside edge (point A) up and over the arm to point B. Measure the arm from front to back, cut fabric, and anchor pin in place.
While tucking the fabric in-between the seat and the arm, you will feel the seat's metal frame. The sides of the metal frame are also attached to the lower inside arms.

30

Mark the fabric where it meets the frame. Cut away this area, leaving about a .5" hem on all three inside cut edges.

Remove arm fabric from the chair and zigzag, or serge, the cut edge. This edge should then be hemmed. Place the arm fabric back on the chair and repeat the same steps on the opposite arm.

31

Tuck the arm fabric around the metal frame and at the back of the arm. Fold up the extra fabric near the wooden cross support, and then pin out the extra fabric on the slope at the back end of the arm. Trim away the excess fabric.

BACK OF
THE ARM

32

Recliner base, seat and arms; lying on the side

Measure and cut the outside arm fabric. Notice how the recliner's outside fabric wraps around the back and is stapled to the inside of the recliner. Now, anchor pin the outside fabric in place. Join the inside and outside arm fabrics together following the manufacturer's seam lines.

NOTE: Do not cut footrest lever opening at this time.

33

The arm's outside roll tapers in size. Pleat out the excess fabric (see arrow).

34

Measure the front arm cap and cut two fabric pieces. Anchor pin them in place. Join the inside and outside arm fabrics to the front arm cap.

35 Remove the arms and sew all the seams together. Trim and zigzag, or serge, seams. Turn them right-side out and place on the proper arms. *Now you can cut the slit for the footrest lever.* Cut a bias strip of fabric and sew it to the right side of the lever slit.

36

When stapling the bias strip around the lever, the left side is tucked under the right.

37

Now we will return to the seat fabric previously set aside: Cut a piece of fabric 6" wide and the width of the seat front plus 2". Pin and seam it to the lower edge of the seat's boxing, across the front and back, 5" to 6" towards the back of the chair. Pin the hem and sew the loop Velcro to the underside. Staple the hook Velcro to the corresponding area under the seat.

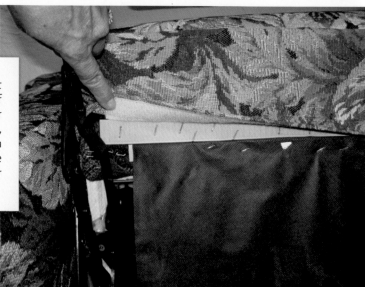

SIDE VIEW OF SEAT	
	TAB

38

Sew a long tab on both lower back corners of the seat. The end of the tab will be stapled or tacked to the lower back arm. The length depends on the recliner.

39

Place arm covers on the recliner and align seams to their proper positions. Staple inside arm covers in place. Now, tip the recliner on its side and staple slipcover along the lower edge of the outside arm; the outside arm fabric wraps around the back of the arm, overlaps the inside arm fabric, and is stapled in place.

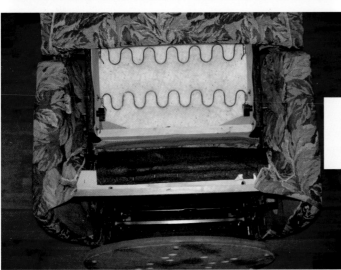

40

Remove the back bolts and place the back into position. Make sure the metal pins are in their proper slots and then put the bolts back in and tighten.

41

Using decorative tacks, fasten the back into position.

Turn the recliner over on its back and open up the footrest. Unscrew the foot and leg rests. Measure fabric to fit the rests and cut, and then zigzag, or serge, the raw edges. Staple the fabric in place. Screw the leg and foot rests back onto the recliner.

Another project finished.

This wooden trimmed recliner belonged to a client's late mother, and she could not bear to part with it. The client requested a slipcover be created for it using her mom's white sheets and tablecloth (for the cording). This was my creation for her, as a remembrance of her mother.

Before

After

Chapter 8

Throw Pillows and More ...

Slipcovers gave new life to these wing back chairs and camel back loveseat. When using two different fabrics in the same room, create a complete look by mixing and matching the throw pillows.

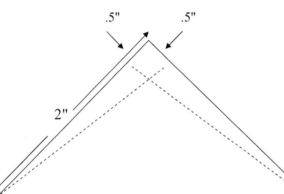

.5"   .5"

2"

1

Cut a front and back for the throw pillow. Taper cut .5" off both sides of all four corners starting 2" back from the corner. The tapering cut will eliminate the pointed corners when the throw pillow is filled.

2 The white cord is made from poly/cotton fibers with a net covering and is washable. Measure the amount of cording needed and cut bias fabric strips. Refer back to chapter 5, "Channel Back Chair," for instructions for making the cording. Starting at the zipper edge, sew the cording to the front of the throw pillow.

3 When sewing the cording to the front pillow fabric, be sure to clip the seam allowance at each corner.

4 To join cording, clip away the extra cord (as shown).

5   Fold the raw edge of the bias strip (see arrow). Position fabric over the corded end and finish stitching to hold the cording joint in place.

6   Fold up .5" to the wrong side on the bottom edge of the back pillow fabric. Place the folded edge over the zipper teeth and pin into place. Now, stitch 1.5" in from the beginning edge and stop 1.5" from the opposite edge. Be sure to back-stitch both ends.

7   Fold back the end of the zipper and clip almost to the fold. Do **NOT** cut past the fold. If you do, the stitching cannot hide the cut.

8   Pin the back to the corded front fabric.

● Back-stitch .25" on the fold (see arrow) and stitch around the pillow. When you reach the opposite end of the zipper/fold area, back-stitch .25" onto the fold. The last step is to pin the zipper to the cording seam allowance and stitch as close to the zipper teeth as possible. Cut away the extra bulk fabric on each corner. Turn the throw pillow right-side out and fill with a pillow insert.

These photos show how throw pillows can add a very nice touch.

1

Do you have a shirt or blouse that would make a funky pillow and complement your bed ensemble or your favorite chair? Follow the directions or put your imagination to work. Cut off the sleeves and then each side seam and both shoulders.

2

Cut the yoke off the top of the shirt back.

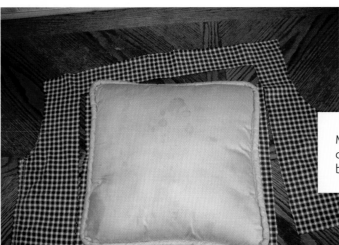

3

Measure the pillow or pillow form to be covered. Cut one surface from the shirt back and attach the zipper.

4

Place the back surface on the front of the shirt and cut it out. This piece is the pillow front. I positioned it so that the buttons were slightly off center and also featured the pocket.

5

Open the sleeve by cutting the under-arm seam and laying it out flat. Cut bias strips for the cording and follow the directions in the Throw Pillow section to complete this shirt pillow.

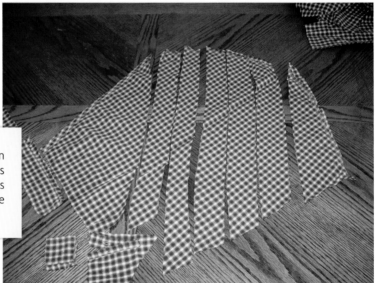

6

To add more character to the pillow, the collar and cuffs could be sewn on the front surface.

Pillow Sham with a Flange

Determine the pillow size needed for your project. Measure the height and width of the pillow and add 9" to each measurement. Divide the 9" as shown below. Transfer the figures to your fabric. If you are using a patterned fabric, be sure to center it. Cut one front for each pillow sham needed.

NOTE: If your fabric is light-weight, a fusible iron on interfacing can be used to give body to your pillow sham.

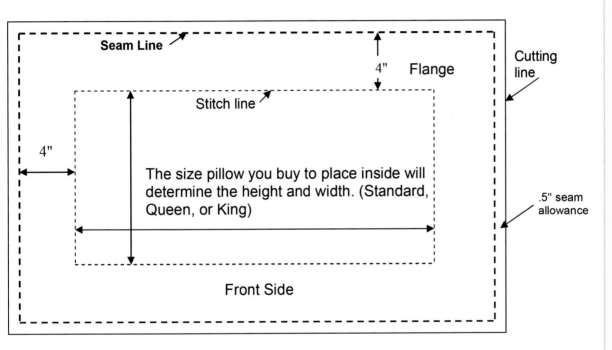

Seam Line

4" Flange

Cutting line

Stitch line

4"

The size pillow you buy to place inside will determine the height and width. (Standard, Queen, or King)

.5" seam allowance

Front Side

BACK OF THE SHAM: Divide the front width measurement in half and add 10" for center back overlap. Cut fabric and hem both overlap edges by folding 1" of the fabric to the wrong side twice and hem. Now you are ready to assemble: Lay front sham right-side up, and lay both back pieces on top of the front face-down.

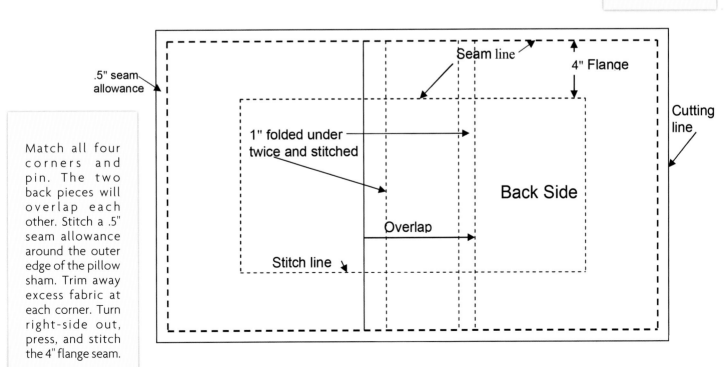

.5" seam allowance

Seam line

4" Flange

1" folded under twice and stitched

Cutting line

Back Side

Overlap

Stitch line

Match all four corners and pin. The two back pieces will overlap each other. Stitch a .5" seam allowance around the outer edge of the pillow sham. Trim away excess fabric at each corner. Turn right-side out, press, and stitch the 4" flange seam.

ENVELOPE PILLOW SHAMS:
Measure pillow and add 1" for seam allowances. Cut one front and one back. Now, cut two flap pieces and add .5" seam allowance on all sides. Place flap pieces right sides together and sew bead trim in-between. Turn right-side out.

Sew cording onto the front section of the sham. To install the zipper, follow the directions in the Throw Pillows section. Sew flap into the top seam, turn right-side out, attach button, and insert pillow.

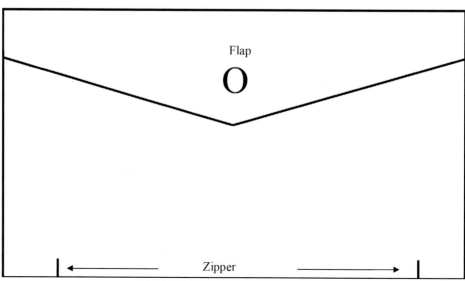

Flap

O

Zipper

Chapter 9

Boxed Cushions for Dining and Kitchen Chairs

Chair seats come in all different shapes and sizes. In order to achieve an excellent fit, make a paper pattern. Most cushions can be made using the directions on the following pages.

These three chair cushions are boxed with two rows of cording and filled with 2" firm foam.

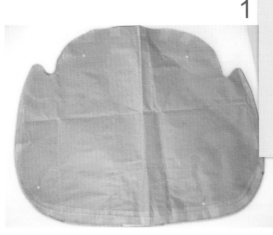

1

Create a paper template using a paper bag, freezer paper, or newspaper. Place paper on the seat and trace the outer edge. Choose two chair rungs and mark with a notch. Notches A and B (see next picture) are for the tab placement. The tabs will fasten around the chair rungs and hold the seat cushion in position. Cut out the template and fold in half. This will assure the right and left sides are identical. If they are not, make the adjustments now. The zipper will start and end at the A and B notches.

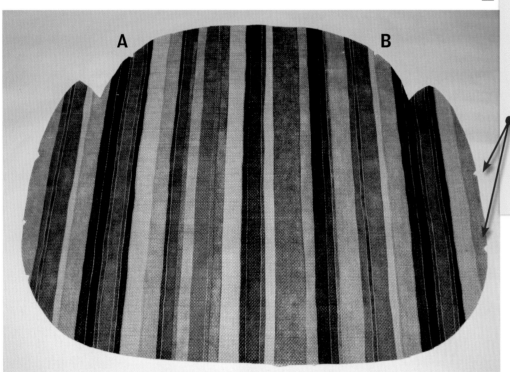

A   B

2

Place template on the fabric, and add .5" for seam allowance to the outer edge before cutting. Cut out two pieces: one top and one bottom. Place both pieces back to back and clip small notches around the outer edge as shown. This will allow proper alignment when sewing the boxing to the second side.

3

To prepare the cording, follow the directions in Chapter 5, "Channel Back Chair." Stitch the cording to both surfaces. Clip cording seam allowance when sewing around the curves.

For this kitchen chair cushion insert, use 2" firm foam, Dacron wrapped, to add plumpness and soften the foam edges. Measure from notch A (refer to previous pictures) around the front of the cushion to notch B and add 4". This will be the length of the boxing strip needed. When using 2" thick foam, you will need to cut boxing 3" wide, allowing for two .5" seam allowances.

4

Cut two fabric strips, one for each side of the zipper. Each piece will be half the width of the boxing plus 1" for turn under, equaling 2.5". The length will be the measurement between notches A and B (back of the cushion plus 2").

5

Measure the length and width of tabs needed and cut four of them. Fold raw edges to the inside of the tab and stitch. Sew one part of the hook and loop Velcro to each tab and then sew them together as shown.

6

It's time to assemble the chair cushion: Fold boxing in half to find center. Mark and pin to the center front of the seat surface, matching stripes. Pin the boxing around the seat cushion toward notches A and B.

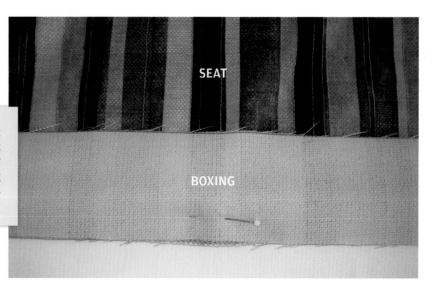

SEAT

BOXING

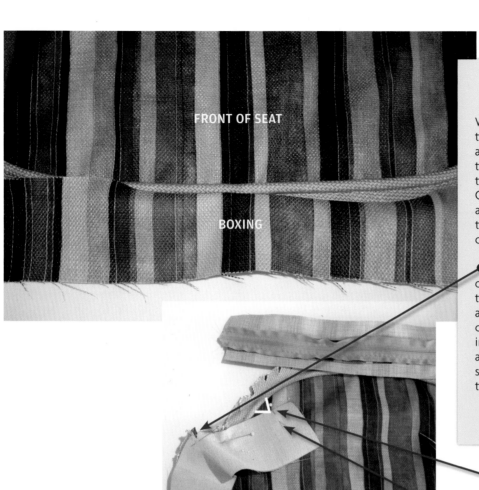

7

FRONT OF SEAT

BOXING

While pinning the boxing to the seat, check the stripe alignment. As you pin around the front curves, eventually the stripes will not match up. Clip the boxing seam allowance as you pin. Continue pinning towards the back corner of the chair cushion.

- At the outside back corner of the cushion cover, clip the boxing seam allowance, and then pin and turn the corner. Pin the boxing to the inside corner. Clip the seam allowance, but do not clip the stitching. Continue pinning towards the zipper (notch A).

Notch A
is where the boxing,
Velcro tabs, and zipper are
joined. Mark with a pin.

8

- Now, repeat all instructions on the opposite side of the chair cushion cover.

9

Place Velcro tabs in the center of the boxing at the zipper/tab notch A mark. Stitch across the end of the tabs to securely hold them in place.

10

Place the end of the boxing Point A over the tabs. Stitch through all layers two or three times to keep the zipper's teeth from pulling apart. If you wish, a small square of fabric can be stitched over the zipper teeth. Always back-stitch the beginning and end of each seam.

11

Mark the opposite end of the boxing at notch B, and stitch the tabs' seam allowance to the center of the boxing at the notch B marking. Pin the zipper's edge to the corded back edge of the chair cushion, towards notch B, and mark with a pin.

12

Join the boxing and zipper end at the markings, and stitch through all layers. Make sure the right and left sides of the zipper teeth stay close together.

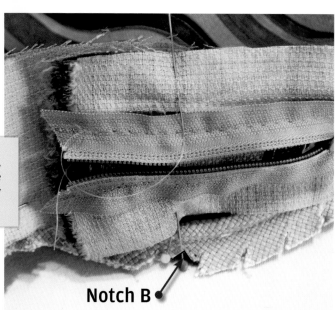

Notch B

13

Check all pinning, making sure the boxing and zipper are securely pinned into place. Stitch around the cushion cover. Turn right-side out and check the seam.

14

Pin the second cushion cover surface to the boxing. Be sure to match stripes in the front and notches at the outer edges. Match zipper notches A and B to the boxing/zipper seams.

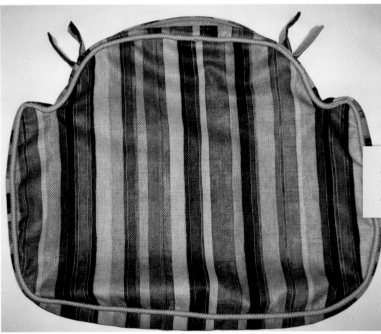

15

Stitch the seam, making any clips where necessary. Turn right-side out and check seams.

16

Lay the paper template on the foam. Place a few anchor pins through the template and into the foam to hold it in place. Trace around the template with a marker. Remove the pins and template.

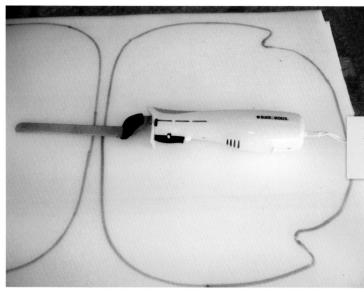

17

The easiest way to cut foam is with an electric knife.

NOTE: Spray the blades with a silicone spray before you begin to cut the foam. Be sure the silicone spray can be used on foam and fabric.

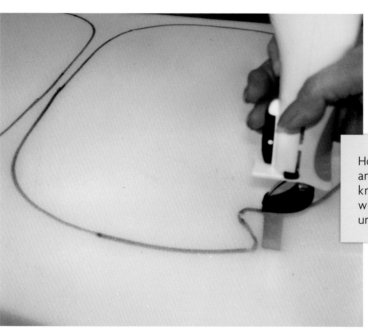

18

Hold the electric knife at a 90-degree angle to the foam. Do NOT tilt the knife from side-to-side, as this will gouge the foam and create an uneven edge.

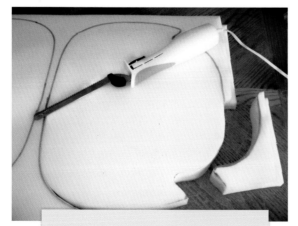

19

Cut away a little foam at a time to prevent the foam trimmings from becoming too heavy, hanging, or distorting the foam's cut edge.

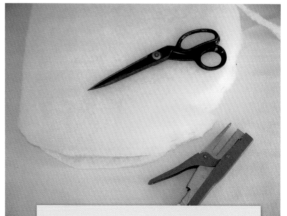

20

Dacron wrapping the foam: Cut top and bottom layers of Dacron about .75" larger than the foam. Place the foam in between the two layers of Dacron.

21 Staple both layers of Dacron at the outermost edge. If your cushion is going to be exposed to the salt air, be sure to use stainless staples or hand-sew the Dacron together.

NOTE: Do NOT staple through the foam.

22 Fold the Dacron-covered foam in half and slide it into your new seat cushion.

23

Reach inside the new cushion cover and adjust the foam. Make sure both seam allowances lay flat against the boxing.

NOTE: If all of the cording seam allowances do not lay in the same direction, it will make the cording appear crooked.

24

Close the zipper and be proud — you have just completed your first chair seat cushion.

Chapter 10

Dining Chairs - Backs

A client called with a plea for "help." Her new kitten liked to climb their new dining room chairs made from woven seagrass. She realized right away that a cover for protection would be needed. As she described her vision, I sketched a picture — it was exactly what she wanted. Because the top of the chair is wider than the base of the back, at seat level, an opening in the back was needed. A tab with buttons embellishes the back closure.

1

In order to slipcover the back of this chair, double-sided tape will be used where you would normally use anchor pins. Measure the height and width of the front/back, extending down 3" to 4" past the top of the seat. Cut the fabric front and tape in place.

2

Measure the height and width of the back. Keep in mind the closure will be in the center of the back; therefore, extra width will be required. Cut two pieces of fabric, a right and left for the back, equaling one-half the width plus 4". Place right sides together and stitch down from the top about 2" and in from the cut edge about 3", depending on serging or hemming requirements.

NOTE: When using the tape, always test in an inconspicuous place, making sure the tape does not leave a mark or damage the paint.

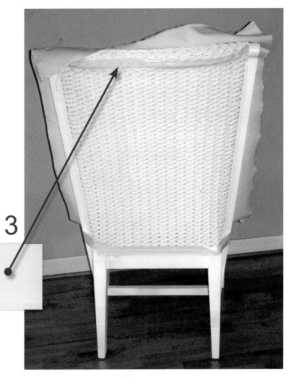

3

Measure and cut the fabric piece required for the top edge of the chair. Tape into place.

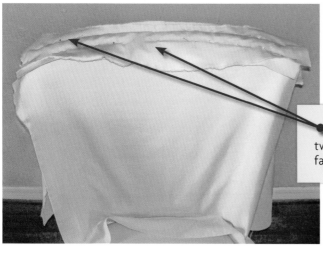

4

Place the back fabric into position. The two seams joining the front, back, and top fabrics together are not corded.

5

Cut two side strips and tape in place. The side seams are the only corded seams. Start at the top of the seat and join the front and side panel with cording in the seam. Continue pinning up the front to the top, clipping the seam allowance as you round the top and pin down towards the back lower edge. Repeat the same process on the opposite side of the chair.

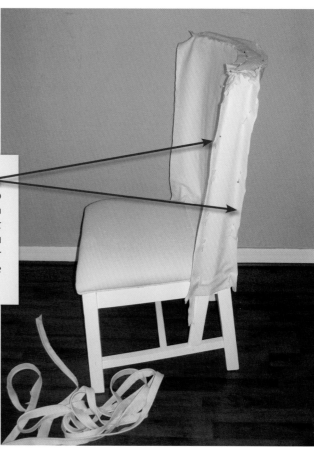

6

Tuck the front fabric in-between the back of the seat and the back. Mark the hemline with pins. Now, remove the cover from the chair and sew all seams. Trim away all extra fabric, leaving about .5" seam allowance. Turn right-side out and try it on the chair. Make any adjustments before zigzagging, or serging, seams.

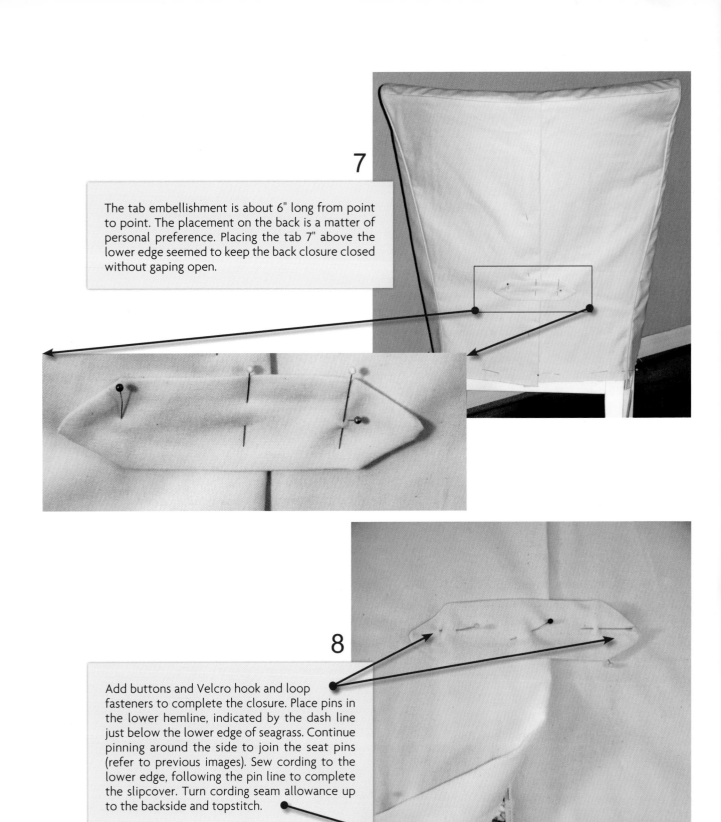

7

The tab embellishment is about 6" long from point to point. The placement on the back is a matter of personal preference. Placing the tab 7" above the lower edge seemed to keep the back closure closed without gaping open.

8

Add buttons and Velcro hook and loop fasteners to complete the closure. Place pins in the lower hemline, indicated by the dash line just below the lower edge of seagrass. Continue pinning around the side to join the seat pins (refer to previous images). Sew cording to the lower edge, following the pin line to complete the slipcover. Turn cording seam allowance up to the backside and topstitch.

Chapter 11

Ceiling to Floor Canopy Over a Bed

The ceiling to floor canopy is made in three sections: The middle teal panel in back of the headboard is gathered on a small diameter aluminum rod and attached to the bottom edge of the 30" wide board with cup hooks. The two floral panels are lined with the teal fabric. Pinch pleats are 5" deep and 5" apart on the top of both floral panels. To join the three-drapery panels, hook and loop pieces of Velcro are sewn intermittently to adjoining drapery edges from ceiling to floor.

The wooden form for the canopy was built out of assorted woods. The top is solid, made from .5" thick MDF board. The front curve is 6" tall and made with a thin sheet of veneer. The straight back is a .5"-thick pine board.

On the top and bottom edges of the front curve, staple the hook Velcro. Sew the loop Velcro to the top backside of the drapery pleats. The underside of the form is completely open for easy mounting to the ceiling and wall. To cover the open underside, create a fabric cover with loop Velcro and staple the straight side to the lower straight edge of the form.

To mount the wooden form to the ceiling/wall, find the wall studs. Place the form up to the ceiling/wall and screw through the form into the studs with 3" screws. After mounting the form to the wall/ceiling, the cover can be put in place, covering the open underside.

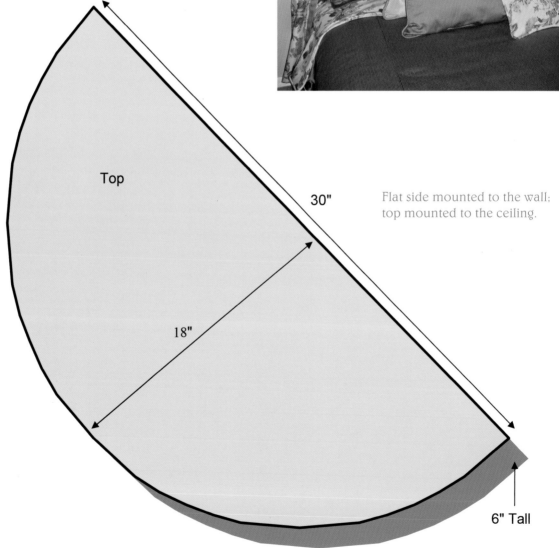

Top

30"

18"

Flat side mounted to the wall; top mounted to the ceiling.

6" Tall

Chapter 12

Neck Rolls

Neck rolls are cylindrical in shape and generally used to accent a bed ensemble, furniture, or window seats. They can be made with gathered ends — the gathering stitches are concealed with covered buttons or decorations of your choice. The small, teal-colored neck rolls (above right) have flat round ends adorned with handmade flowerets and a covered button in the center.

To get started, measure the size neck rolls you need and purchase the roll insert at your local fabric store, or create your own insert using muslin or drapery lining fabric and fiberfill stuffing. For this project, the neck roll insert measures 20" in length and 9" in diameter. The width of the cut fabric will be 21", with 1" allowed for seam allowances. The length is determined by measuring the circumference (29") of the neck roll plus allowing 1.5" for the zipper seam allowances, equaling 30.5".

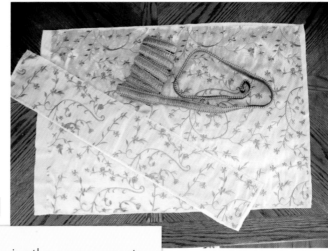

1

Cut the main body fabric using these measurements. Also cut two strips, one for each end of the neck roll. The width is half the diameter plus 1" for seam allowance and gathering at the ends equaling 5.5". The length is 30.5".

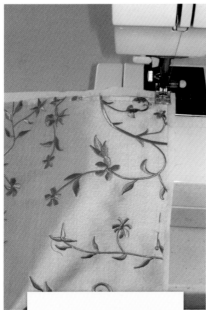

2 This fabric — lightweight, embroidered silk — will be lined with drapery lining fabric. Lay all neck roll pieces on the lining, pin through both layers, and cut them out. Zigzag or serge all edges to hold the layers together and to prevent unraveling.

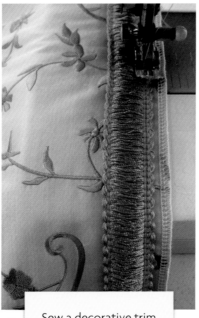

3 Sew a decorative trim or cording to each end of the main body of the fabric.

4 Now, sew the end strips to each end, covering the trim.

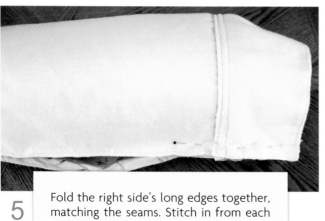

5 Fold the right side's long edges together, matching the seams. Stitch in from each end over seam allowance and back-stitch. Leave about 17" to 18" open for the zipper.

6 Pull the chain stitch holding the trim's outer edge together.

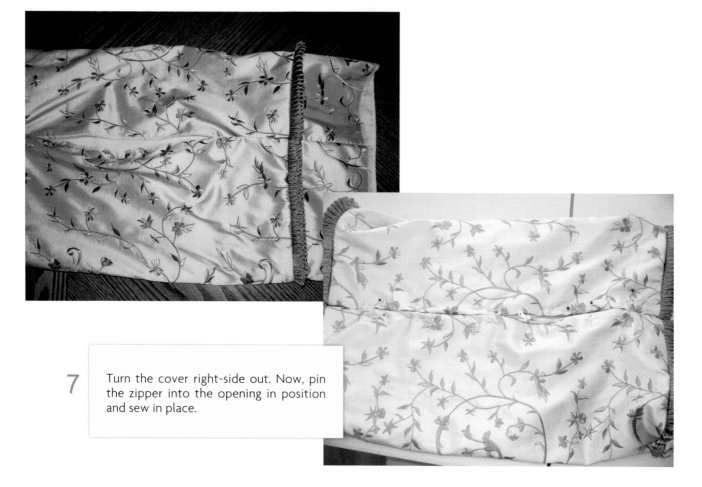

7 Turn the cover right-side out. Now, pin the zipper into the opening in position and sew in place.

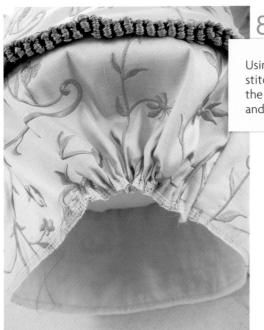

 8

Using a strong thread, hand-sew a running stitch at both ends. Pull on both ends of the thread to create the tight gathering and tie thread securely.

9

Cover large buttons with the neck roll fabric, or a contrasting fabric could be used. Attach the buttons with hot glue, covering the gathering threads.

My client designed these neck rolls. Cut out the neck roll circular ends and stitch covered cording to the outer edges. Measure the outside circumference — this measurement will dictate the height of the fabric pieces needed. The length of the roll will be determined by the width of the fabric pieces.

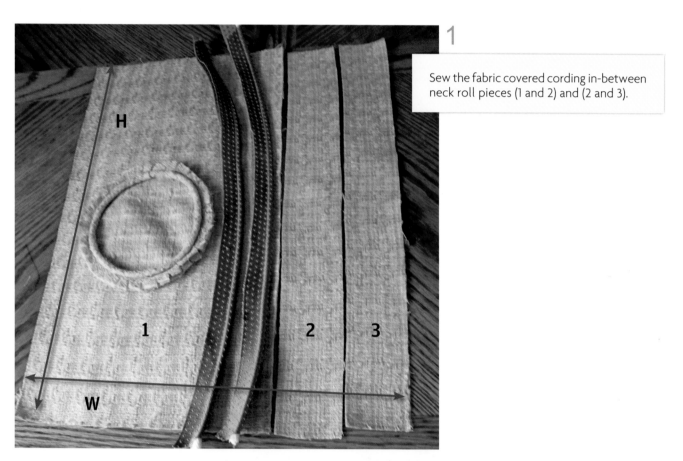

1

Sew the fabric covered cording in-between neck roll pieces (1 and 2) and (2 and 3).

2

Fold the main body in half, matching the cording and seam. Leave a small opening for stuffing. Divide the main body ends into fourths and mark with pins. Repeat this step with the circle ends.

3   Pin the main body to the end circles, matching pins, and then sew the seam. Repeat this step on the remaining ends. Turn right-side out and inspect all seams.

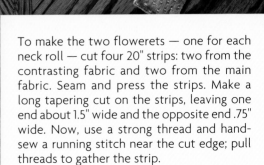

4   To make the two flowerets — one for each neck roll — cut four 20" strips: two from the contrasting fabric and two from the main fabric. Seam and press the strips. Make a long tapering cut on the strips, leaving one end about 1.5" wide and the opposite end .75" wide. Now, use a strong thread and hand-sew a running stitch near the cut edge; pull threads to gather the strip.

5

Twist the gathered strip into a floweret, and hot glue it together. Now, hot glue the floweret and covered button to the end of the neck roll. Stuff with fiberfill and hand-sew together.

Chapter 13

Sectionals

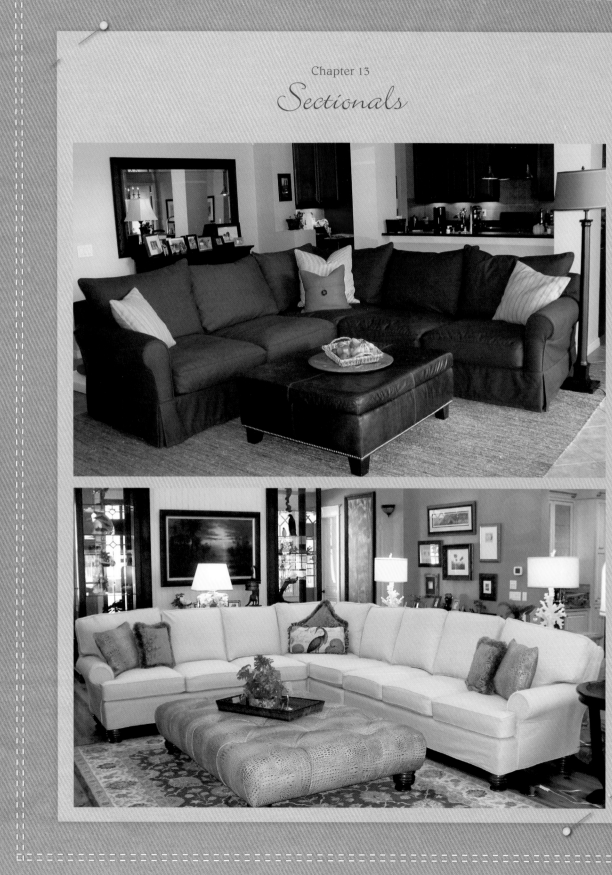

This sectional sofa is a bit more complicated because some of the fitting will need to be completed right-side out. Sections 2 and 3 can be fitted wrong-side out because their ends are identical. Notice that sections 1 and 4 have only one arm each, so they will need to be fitted slightly differently.

Sections 1 and 4: Backs and arms measure the same dimensions. The inside backs/arms, outside backs/arms, and arm fronts of both are pin fitted wrong-side out. After pin fitting each back/arm section, slide them off and sew together. Turn section 4 right-side out and place it on section 1. Turn section 1 right-side out and place it on section 4. The remainder of these two pieces — the decking and front edges — will be finished right-side out.

The seat cushions for all sections are fitted wrong-side out. They all have a single horizontal row of cording across the center and pleats at the front corners. At the end of this chapter, you will be shown how to fit them (see page 102).

With time and patience, you could create a slipcover like this one. Yardage required will be approximately 38 to 42 yards, depending on pattern repeat and/or adding a skirt.

This chocolate brown sectional is fitted wrong-side out. When all three slipcovers are sewn together and turned right-side out, the right love seat slipcover will fit the left love seat. The same is true for the left slipcover; it will be placed on the right love seat. The corner unit is identical on both ends; therefore, the slipcover will fit properly when turned right-side out.

This leather sectional is slip-covered in off-white linen and consists of two one-armed sofas, one single chair, and one corner piece. The corner and single armless chair sections are the same on both of their side/ends; therefore, they can be pin-fitted wrong-side out. Because the two one-armed sofas are mirror images of one another, each piece can also be fitted wrong-side out. After the slipcovers are sewn together and turned right-side out, the slipcover pin-fitted on the left sofa will be placed on the right sofa and the slipcover pin-fitted on the right sofa will be placed on the left sofa. Staple the hook Velcro to the lower bottom edge of the sectional and sew loop Velcro to the cording seam allowance at the lower edge of each slipcover.

This slip-covering project also included a set of plaid cushion covers, which will give my client five different decorating combinations: the original chocolate brown leather, brown leather with the off-white linen cushion covers, brown leather with the plaid cushion covers, plaid covers with the off-white linen slipcover, and the complete off-white linen slipcover set shown here.

To pin-fit a shabby chic slipcover, follow the techniques shown in this book that pertain to your style of furniture, but pin a bit looser. The client requested the skirt be longer and drape on the floor. The length of the skirt is purely a personal preference. Refer to the following page for instructions on how to pin-fit the cushions (shown above) wrong-side out.

Pinning A Cushion Wrong-Side Out

1 Lay fabric on right-side facing cushion and the top and bottom of the cushion, and anchor pin them in place. Trim away excess fabric, leaving enough for seam allowances.

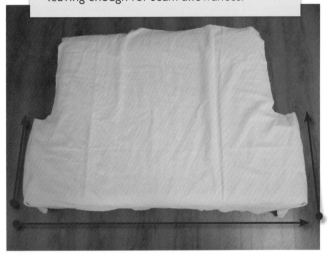

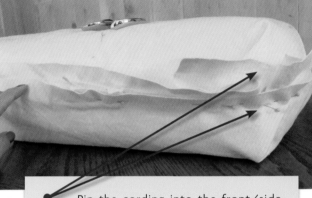

2 Pin the cording into the front/side seam following the manufacturer's cording. Fold extra fabric into a pleat at the corners.

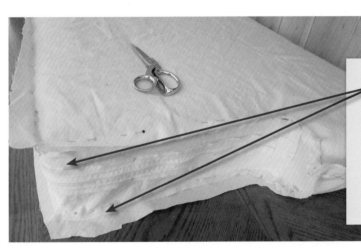

3 Measure the length of the zipper needed; be sure to extend it well around the corners for easy cushion removal. Cut two fabric strips — one for each side of the zipper — and sew them onto the zipper. Now, anchor pin the zipper directly over the cushion's zipper and add a piece of fabric to complete the boxing. Join the top and bottom cushion fabrics to the strips sewn to the right and left sides of the zipper and the extra boxing fabric.

4 Remove anchor pins and unzip the zipper. Slide the cushion out of the newly-pinned cushion cover, sew all seams, turn right-side out, and try it on the cushion. If there are any adjustments to be made, now is the time to do so. Trim seam allowance and zigzag or serge all seams to prevent unraveling when cleaning.

Chapter 14

Sleeper Sofa with Attached Back Cushions

This sofa is an older style with attached back cushions. I suggested to the client that she allow me to detach them and slipcover each cushion separately.

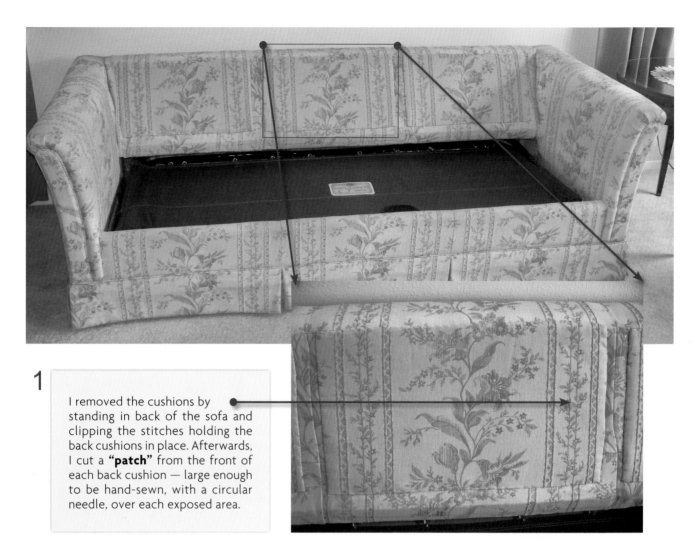

1 I removed the cushions by standing in back of the sofa and clipping the stitches holding the back cushions in place. Afterwards, I cut a **"patch"** from the front of each back cushion — large enough to be hand-sewn, with a circular needle, over each exposed area.

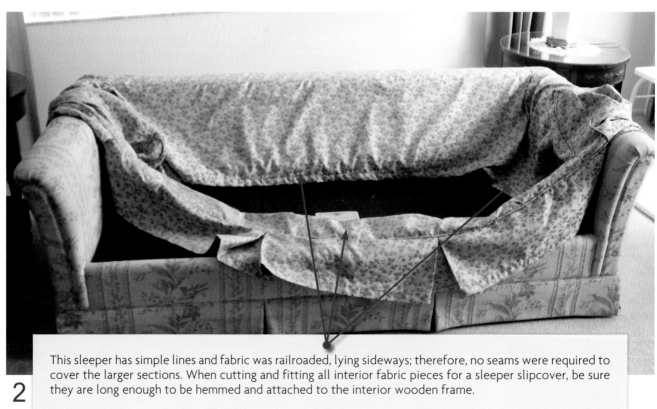

2 This sleeper has simple lines and fabric was railroaded, lying sideways; therefore, no seams were required to cover the larger sections. When cutting and fitting all interior fabric pieces for a sleeper slipcover, be sure they are long enough to be hemmed and attached to the interior wooden frame.

3

To attach a sleeper slipcover, start at both top back corners and slide the arms into position one at a time.

4

After the slipcover is completely in place, hold both sides of the zipper close together to relieve any stress while sliding the zipper closed.

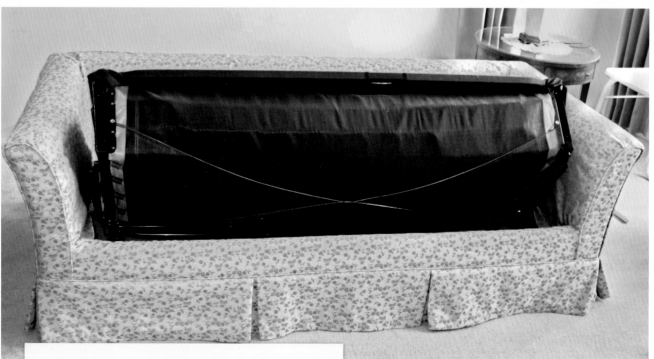

5 Velcro, staple, or tack the interior perimeter to the corresponding wooden frame.

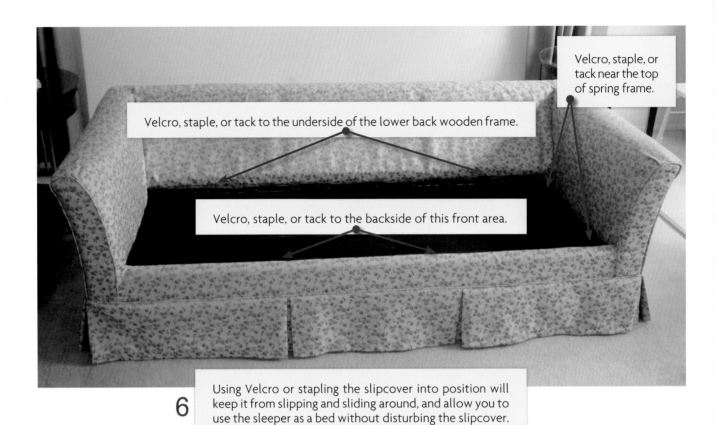

Velcro, staple, or tack near the top of spring frame.

Velcro, staple, or tack to the underside of the lower back wooden frame.

Velcro, staple, or tack to the backside of this front area.

6   Using Velcro or stapling the slipcover into position will keep it from slipping and sliding around, and allow you to use the sleeper as a bed without disturbing the slipcover.

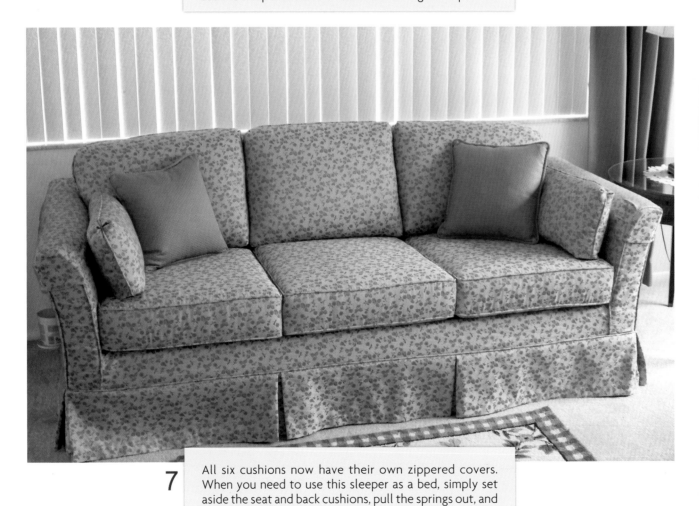

7   All six cushions now have their own zippered covers. When you need to use this sleeper as a bed, simply set aside the seat and back cushions, pull the springs out, and unfold the bed.

Chapter 15

Slip-covering a Wooden-trimmed Chair

My theory, after thirty-nine years of upholstering and creating custom slipcovers, is that most all pieces of furniture can be slip-covered, including this one with the wood trim. My suggestion is: the fabric needs to be medium to heavy upholstery weight — for example, tapestries, velvets, and chenille — but it needs to be soft and pliable.

NOTE: A tall/long tailored or gathered skirt could be added to this chair, changing the style once again.

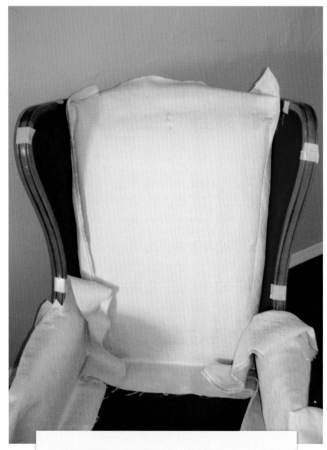

1 Use double-sided tape to adhere fabric to the wood.

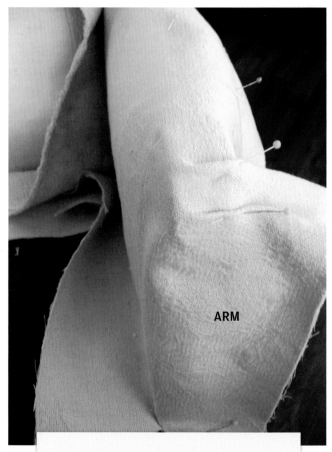

ARM

2 Pin out the excess fabric by creating small darts on the front of each arm.

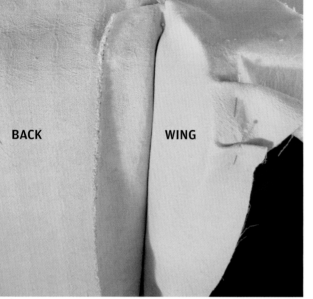

BACK

WING

 3

Pin out the excess fabric at the top/front of the wing.

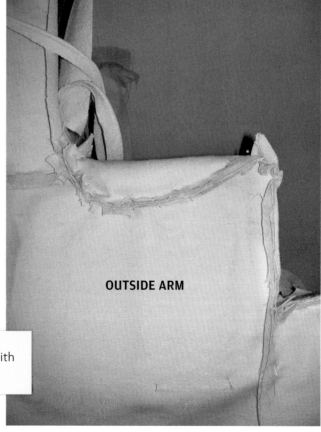

OUTSIDE ARM

4

Follow the manufacturer's seam lines with the cording.

Chapter 16

Reusing Drapes

A client had a large pair of floor-to-ceiling floral drapes and wanted to reuse them. As he described his vision, I made a sketch that met his approval. I dismantled, serged, and laundered all of the panels and, from the panels, I made a coverlet for a single platform bed, a pillow sham, a scarf valance, and the Roman shade. All are corded in a contrasting cream fabric, and the drape is a coordinating fabric as well. The rosettes are long strips of fabric hand-gathered and hot-glued onto a wooden circle. The circle is attached to a 7" section of dowel 1" in diameter. At the end of the dowel a hole is drilled and a double-ended screw is inserted.

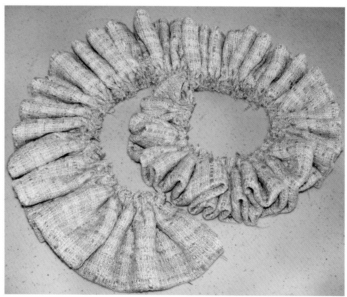

Gathering line .... 6"

3"   3 yards long

Fold

The size of the rosette is determined by the width of the fabric strip. My strip is about 3 yards long and 13" wide. Fold the strip in half lengthwise and hand-gather with a strong thread at an angle. Trim away extra fabric after hand-sewing and before gathering. (See page 116 to complete the rosettes.)

FOLD

1

ROMAN SHADE: The window measures 51.25" wide inside, casing-to-casing. Each dismantled drape had two and a half panels. Only one panel is used for the shade without having to seam the fabric. I pressed and folded one full width panel in half lengthwise; then I drew the shape at the bottom of the shade and cut. Make cording following the instructions in Chapter 4 and sew it to the bottom edge of the shade.

2

Clip all of the curves. Lay the lining and interlining in place and pin and sew all layers together.

3

After trimming the seam allowance, turn the shade right-side out, check the seam, and press.

4

Measure and then trim away excess lining and interlining fabrics to the desired finished shade width of 51.25". Hem both sides by folding the surface fabric over the linings, turning under raw edge and stitch.

5

On the lining side, measure up 5" from the lower corners and mark with pins. This will allow the sculptured edge to hang below the first 4" horizontal pleat. Place a long measuring device across the shade, touching both pins. Divide the measurement by three; this will give you four equal vertical rows.

1	2	3	4

Roman shade drawing.

8"

6

Measure the four rows up towards the top of the shade, placing the pins at 8" intervals.

7

Hand-sew or zigzag a plastic ring to each pin placement on the lining side. I have blue thread in the bobbin and white thread on top of the sewing machine. When installing the Roman shade, lift cords will be strung through each row of the rings, starting at the top of the shade. These cords will raise and lower the shade. When the shade is raised, the 8" section in between each ring will create 4" horizontal folds.

Note: Plastic rings and lift cord can be purchased at most fabric stores.

8

I am using a 1" thick pine board for the inside mount of the Roman shade. Wrap it with drapery lining fabric and staple in place. Staple the hook Velcro the full length of the board, about 1" away from the front edge, and sew loop Velcro to the top back edge of the shade. Turn the board over and install a screw eye opposite each of the first three vertical rows of rings starting on the left for a right-hand lift.

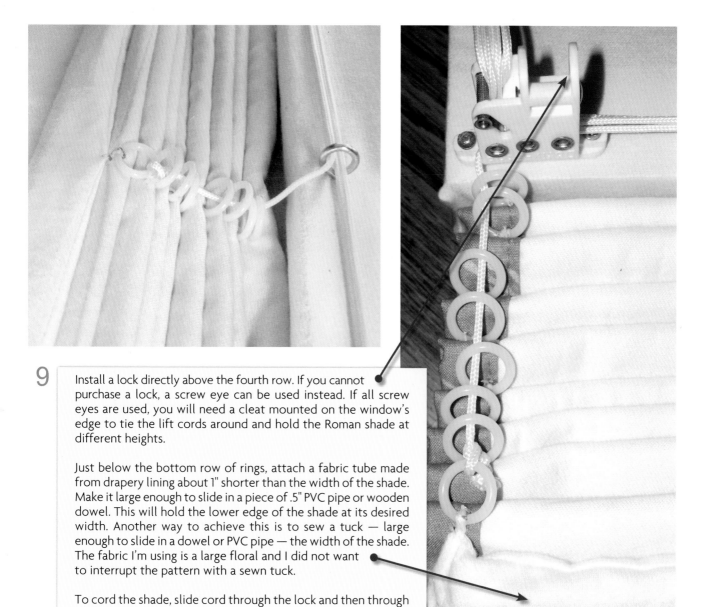

9 Install a lock directly above the fourth row. If you cannot purchase a lock, a screw eye can be used instead. If all screw eyes are used, you will need a cleat mounted on the window's edge to tie the lift cords around and hold the Roman shade at different heights.

Just below the bottom row of rings, attach a fabric tube made from drapery lining about 1" shorter than the width of the shade. Make it large enough to slide in a piece of .5" PVC pipe or wooden dowel. This will hold the lower edge of the shade at its desired width. Another way to achieve this is to sew a tuck — large enough to slide in a dowel or PVC pipe — the width of the shade. The fabric I'm using is a large floral and I did not want to interrupt the pattern with a sewn tuck.

To cord the shade, slide cord through the lock and then through all three screw eyes. Continue towards the bottom of the shade, threading through all of the rings. Knot the cord at the last ring. Pull shade flat and cut the cord past the lock, leaving two to three yards. Excess cord can be trimmed away after the Roman shade has been installed.

Note: A small amount of hot glue on each knot will ensure the knots will not loosen or untie.

Making Fabric Rosettes

Hot glue the gathered strip to the wood circle. Start in the center and continue gluing in a circle, behind the previous row.

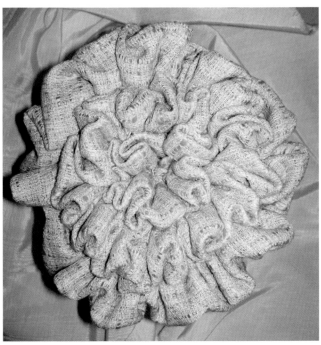

The button in the center of the rosette is covered with the same fabric used to make the cording for the lower edge of the Roman shade.

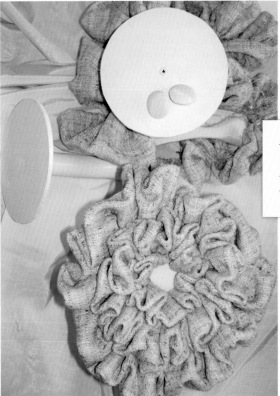

Chapter 17

Adding to Shabby Chic

For this project, two standard pillow shams were transformed into larger Euro shams with ruffles and two table runners into the iron bed canopy valance.

Changing Table Runner to Chic Bedroom Valance

The client showed me two antique table runners and described the look she wanted for her bed valance. The look was achieved by overlapping the runners about 2", stitching a gathering thread 2.5" from the top edge and gathering it to the dimensions needed. Next, a .75" loop Velcro was stitched to the front side while self-sticking hook Velcro was secured to the backside of the top iron valance rail of the bed. Once the converted table runners were added, it created a very nice valance for the antique iron bed.

Changing Standard Shams to Euro Shams with Ruffles

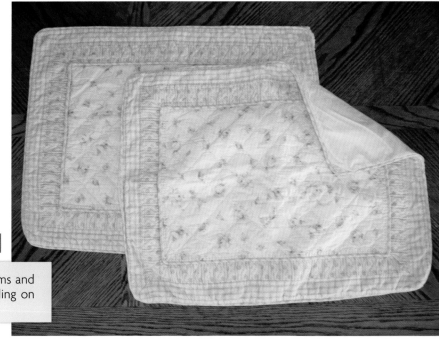

1

Start with two standard pillow shams and remove the backs, leaving the cording on the outer edge.

2   Next, cut white fabric into 3.5" wide strips and sew them on all four sides of each sham, mitering the corners.

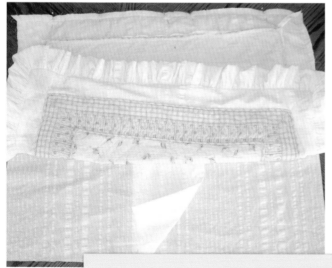

3   Add the ruffle by cutting 6" wide strips and sewing them together end-to-end. Next, fold the strips in half lengthwise and gather. Attach the gathered strip to the outer perimeter of both sham fronts. Now, cut four back pieces, hem the leading edges (as shown), overlap, and sew to the front side of each Euro sham. Turn right-side out and fill with a pillow insert.

Chapter 18

Bathroom and Kitchen Accessories

Towel Bar

The bathroom towel bar drape was the brainchild of a client, and I have to admit it's a very nice embellishment in her guest bathroom. The tapestry fabric was purchased as a remnant. She told me her vision, and my first thought was that it would need to be cleaned often. Therefore, the closure over the towel bar would need to be simple and easy to assemble.

Closure choices were Velcro, snaps, or buttons. Her choice was Velcro. The towel bar drape is lined with velvet and trimmed with a tassel fringe.

The width of the drape is the width of the towel bar in-between the brackets, plus seam allowances. The length is a matter of preference based on the size of the towels to be used. To the right are approximate dimensions used.

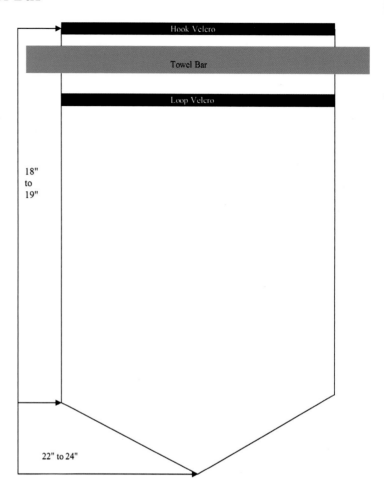

Hook Velcro

Towel Bar

Loop Velcro

18" to 19"

22" to 24"

Banquettes

Custom-made banquettes require custom cut foam and cushion covers. I recommend 4" to 5" thick firm foam for seats and 4" soft foam for the back cushions. Dacron wrapping the cushions is always a good idea because it softens the sharp 90-degree angles on the edges of the foam. Foam can be purchased at most fabric stores. When measuring for the foam needed, add .5" extra to the side-to-side and front to back measurements. Yellow chair cushions on previous page have a 2" firm foam insert with Velcro tabs to secure to the chair.

This custom kitchen banquette was built from black Formica with rounded outside corners and has an inside curve at the corner of the banquette. When planning the layout of the cushions, I used paper taped together to make it large enough to cover the entire seating area. To maximize use of the bottom cushions, each end cushion is the same shape and dimension, allowing them to be swapped. The cushion in the inside corner area is the same dimension on both sides, making it possible to be flipped in position, and the fourth cushion fills in the remaining area. The back cushions have Velcro to hold them to the backrest; 5" firm foam was used for the seating area and 4" soft foam for the back cushions.

Chapter 19

Valances

All of these valances start with a long, lined, strip of fabric. It depends on how you fold, pleat, tuck, trim, embellish, or gather that creates the style. I hardly ever use a pattern to create a valance. The client explains their vision or shows me a picture from a magazine. Sometimes they are not sure what they want and leave it up to me. I study the fabric's pattern and sketch what I envision.

Opposite Page: The red and white stripe valance is pleated horizontally and pleats are hand-sewn in place. The yellow valance is finished with tabs and embellished with contrasting fabric-covered buttons. The red/teal floral valances are mounted on 1" x 4" boards, with "L"-shaped brackets creating a shelf, and has vertical fabric bands holding pleats in place. The chocolate brown/gold floral valance is simply gathered and sewn onto a flat fabric band and tacked onto a 1" x 4" board, with "L"-shaped brackets creating a shelf.

My suggestion to you: Be original and create your own one-of-a-kind valance.

Pretty in Peach

Following the pattern creates the shape of this valance's lower edge. It is mounted on a 1" pine board wrapped with drapery lining, and is attached to the wall with metal "L"-shaped brackets.

The chair cushions are filled with 2" firm foam, and have Velcro tabs to secure them to the chair. To make chair cushions, follow the instructions in chapter 9, "Boxed Cushions."

Placemats are shaped to fit the round table. With newspaper or a brown bag for a template, you can create your own placemats. Again, be creative.

From the Dining Room Window to the Bathroom

The dining room window consisted of one large center window and two narrow windows. Each window had a single Roman valance mounted inside the window frame; one small valance fit perfectly in the small bathroom window while a creative use was found for the remaining two valances.

The remaining two valances are being remade into a Roman valance to top the client's shower curtain.

The second small valance is taken apart and cut into three sections. Save the plastic rings and trim to use later. Release the outer edge hems of the large valance. The two outside sections (1 and 2), including lining, are added to the outer edges of the large valance (3). Hem both outside edges to the desired width. The center section is cut and sewn into two long ties to hold back the two halves of the shower curtain.

3 Hem the bottom edge. Reattach the ball fringe trim, using the trim removed from the small valance, to extend the trim across the added width.

4 When joining the trim, fold under the cut edge, matching the design so it appears continuous.

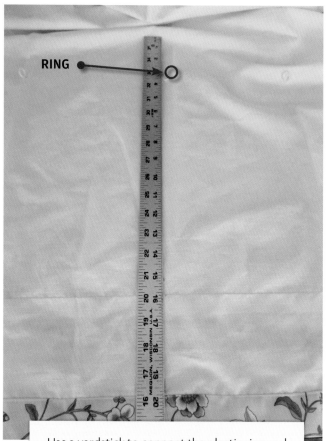

RING

5 Use a yardstick to connect the plastic ring and the original ring mark to find the new location for the ring on the outside hem.

Bathroom transformed.

1

Use 1" x 4" pine boards and follow your angle diagram to find and cut the angles. Cover the three sections with lining fabric.

ANGLE FINDER

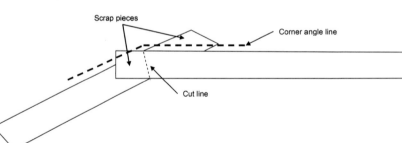

Scrap pieces

Corner angle line

Cut line

2 The valance boards are mounted to the wall with metal "L"-shaped brackets. To assemble the valance, metal cleat the valance boards together as shown in photo. This will aid in positioning and pleating the valance sections. To transport the valance to the client's home, I removed the cleats, unpinned the right and left sides, and folded and secured them to the center.

3

I let the fabric design dictate the style of the valance. I divided the valance boards into four sections, (1 right, 1 left, and 2 sections on the center board), divided each section in half and marked with a pin, and then cut four center sections with a curve at the lower edge following the pattern. I then cut five pleat sections.

4

Alternate the sections, starting and ending with a pleat section. Sew all sections together and press seams. Lay sewn sections face down on lining fabric and sew across the bottom, turn right side out, and press.

Now, pin center of each curved section to the half markings on the boards. Secure the center section right and left of center. Pleat evenly the remaining fabric. The valance ends can be finished by hand-hemming. When you have completed all pleating and pinning, remove valance from the valance boards, keeping pins securely holding pleats in proper position.

Sew a 5" fabric band across the top of the valance. Fold fabric band to the backside, turn under raw edge, and stitch in place. The fabric band is used to attach the valance to the top of the valance boards and will not show. Press and reattach valance to the valance boards with tacks or staples.

127

Afterword

To all my sewing friends, who create beautiful quilts, sew prom gowns, sew clothing for your work place, curtains for your home, clothing for your infant/toddler/teen, and maybe your granddaughter's wedding gown — why stop there? Why not try slipcovering that chair your parents passed down to you, the sofa the cat turned to shreds, the rocking chair you rocked your babies in, or the patio cushions.

If you can sew any of the items mentioned, you certainly have the skills it takes to create your own custom slipcover. It is not a daunting task.

I suggest, for your first slipcover project, use sheets from your local thrift store or painters' drop cloths that have become the fabric of choice in my central Florida area. To preshrink the drop cloths, wash in hot water with clear detergent and fabric softener, and then dry on high heat and fold immediately. This will allow you to gain experience and confidence without spending a lot of money.

Give it a try — I know you can create your own beautiful custom slipcover, like those wonderful shirts, pants, and dresses you learned to make years ago. Just don't give up. With patience and practice, you will achieve your goal.